THE FUTURE

FLORENCE GAUB

The Future

A User's Guide

HURST & COMPANY, LONDON

First published in the United Kingdom in 2026 by
C. Hurst & Co. (Publishers) Ltd.,
New Wing, Somerset House, Strand, London, WC2R 1LA
© Florence Gaub, 2026
All rights reserved.

The right of Florence Gaub to be identified
as the author of this publication is asserted by her in accordance
with the Copyright, Designs and Patents Act, 1988.

© 2023 by dtv Verlagsgesellschaft mbH und Co. KG, Munich, Germany.

Distributed in the United States, Canada and Latin America by
Oxford University Press, 546 Fifth Avenue, New York, NY 10036,
United States of America.

A Cataloguing-in-Publication data record for this book
is available from the British Library.

ISBN: 9781805265610

EU GPSR Authorised Representative
Easy Access System Europe Oü, 16879218
Address: Mustamäe tee 50, 10621, Tallinn, Estonia
Contact Details: gpsr.requests@easproject.com, +358 40 500 3575

Printed and bound in Great Britain by Bell & Bain Ltd, Glasgow

www.hurstpublishers.com

CONTENTS

Introduction: Before First Use		1
1.	Technical Specifications	21
	1.1 Characteristics	22
	1.2 Intended use: What is the future for?	28
	1.3 Typologies: Types of futures	34
	1.4 Origins: The history of the future	46
2.	The Functions of Each Part	57
	2.1 The power button	57
	2.2 The present	65
	2.3 The past	72
	2.4 Thinking the new	79
3.	How to Use It	87
	3.1 Almost certainly: What we know	88
	3.2 Live with danger	96
	3.3 Imagine the best	105
	3.4 Live with surprise	113
4.	Safety Instructions: What Not to Do	121
	4.1 Catastrophising	122

	4.2	Wishful thinking	128
	4.3	The illusion of certainty	134
	4.4	Fake futures	143
5.	Troubleshooting		151
	5.1	When the future has expired	152
	5.2	When we cannot see the future	159
	5.3	When the future is bad	166
	5.4	When we do not know what to fill the future with	174
6.	Your Future Warranty		181

Notes   185

INTRODUCTION
BEFORE FIRST USE

For most people, the future is something consumed like lollipops and TV series, passively ingested or watched. They buy off-the-shelf futures from politicians, tech entrepreneurs, science fiction films, religious leaders and psychics to get at least some sense of what could lie ahead. The future is not only viewed as something far away and not here yet but also separate from us and unreal, something that happens all by itself—not unlike an asteroid hurtling towards Earth. However, this perception is wrong.

'The future' isn't distant but something that all humans generate all the time. Individuals do it as much as countries, companies or football clubs. Their futures come with detailed mental images, sounds, even tastes, and although we use the singular, the future always comes as a plural: the possible, the probable, the plausible and even the impossible are all versions of the future we entertain. Instead of being a time far away, the future is everything imaginable about it.

It therefore is already here—permanently. This capacity to mentally travel to a time that is not the present moment is a human capacity unrivalled in the animal kingdom—a little like a superpower, or to go even further, perhaps one of the key features of being human at all. Pretty much everything that makes us human—thinking about choices, making decisions, dreaming, goal setting and worrying—is a form of the future.

Yet most people rarely make full use of this capacity. We might spend half of our waking hours thinking about the future, but most of it goes to rather mundane tasks. The daily future—such as what to eat, when to go to work and how our children's upcoming exams will go—takes up 80% of our thinking about the future. At 14%, looking ahead to the coming year—holidays to take, projects to accomplish and doctor's visits to dread—comes a distant second. Finally, a mere 6% of our time imagining the future concerns the next 10–15 years—thinking about life goals, daydreaming about a possible wedding, a house we want to build or a skill we want to learn.[1] The bigger and more distant future is rarely visited, and when it is, it is quickly abandoned for fear and worry, almost as if it belongs to somebody else or is outside the realm of personal responsibility.

In part, this is due to the misperception that this bigger, collective future is fundamentally different from the personal, small future. The former belongs to governments and companies and is handled with

INTRODUCTION

strategic foresight reports and big data modelling, and the latter with diaries and vision boards—or so the reasoning goes. Books for the former are to be found in the science and tech section, and those for the latter in the self-help section, but this distinction is wrong. All futures are related, stacked into each other like Russian dolls: the daily future is embedded in the personal future, which is part of the future of this era, which is part of the future of the planet. Not only do they depend on each other, but they are all generated in the minds of humans in pretty much the same way: using data from the past, information from the present, and imagination to come up with something new. Every human is capable of all four of them, but most neglect two, often three, of the four available futures; instead of producing the future oneself, one buys futures 'produced' by others.

There are three main reasons why parts of the future have been neglected so far, by individuals, but also by philosophers, politicians and scientists: the necessary skills are not being taught; the future has only recently been discovered by science, and right now, the future appears to be in crisis.

That's where a user's guide comes in.

The sleeping superpower

All humans are born with the cognitive capacity to time travel to multiple and even distant futures; however, excelling at it does not come naturally and therefore must be learnt. Firstly, our day-to-day keeps us anchored in the present as that is where our lives take place; hence, most of our attention goes to the daily future. Travelling further—be it to the personal future or the future of society and the planet—happens less often as it requires more of an active effort; it also requires method and skill as well as a society that encourages and teaches both.

Part of the problem is that most Western societies are structurally more past- than future-oriented, making this task difficult. Educational systems, for instance, focus on skills and disciplines that are less likely to produce innovative ideas. The dominant form of thinking taught in schools is convergent (where logic is used to find one right answer) rather than divergent (where imagination is used to produce as many solutions as possible). History, rather than a futuristic methodology, is mandatory in school. Latin gets more attention than space travel. There are 2,340 history professors in the United States, but only ten professors that teach strategic foresight.

Subjects that foster the capacity to imagine the future, such as the arts, literature, philosophy, or—shocking—the art of doing nothing are often seen as second-rate disciplines, useless on the labour market.

This penchant for the past can be found elsewhere, too. In psychology, the dominant current still seeks to find the cause of problems in the patient's past rather

INTRODUCTION

than searching for a solution in their future. Religions have not been of much assistance either: the monotheistic ones want humanity to return to the past, to a paradise lost. Of course, the twenty-first century and its addiction to the instant future—tweets, quarterly reports and election cycles—promotes supreme short-termism and what is called 'future discounting', the practice of 'taking out loans' on the future to solve problems in the present. (Some also call it the practice of colonising the future, or to take something that is not ours by force.) Culture plays a role, too: Western ones tend to be collectively less drawn to the future than Asian ones.[2] Structurally, our society is therefore poorly future-oriented; we have no tools to help people to generate the future by themselves, for example, at school or university. However, this is not the only reason why we neglect the future.

Future horizons

Public future	Measures of time	Personal future
Quiz shows Stock markets Public auctions Tweeting	Seconds	Texting 1-click buying Cycle of breath
Traffic lights Public transport 24/7 news Emergency response	Minutes	Emailing Taking a shower Coffee break

THE FUTURE

Public future	**Measures of time**	**Personal future**
Opening hours Parking meters Appointments	Hours	Work shift Sunday lunch Phone battery
Daily newspapers Discount sales Music festivals	Days	Postage Weekly shop Exercise classes
Quarterly reporting Fashion fads Software updates	Months	School term Pregnancy Diet
Trade negotiations Olympic Games Election cycles	Years	College degree Career plans Raising children
Space programmes Energy transitions Chinese planning	Decades	Mortgage Pension saving Making a will
Cathedral building Generational thinking Seed banks	Centuries	Planting an oak tree Time capsules Belief in the afterlife

Source: Adapted from *The Good Ancestor* by Roman Krznaric, p. 33.

Discovery of the future

Our structural inclination towards the present and the past is also rooted in the fact that, until recently, the future had not been studied extensively.

INTRODUCTION

Historically, humans had not thought of the future as something that was created in their heads, shaped by their decisions, dreams and fears. Instead, they had considered the future to have been created by somebody else, and all they could do was watch it unfold. The reason was that for most of them, their influence on the future was limited to their personal lives. However, the future was not really a space of possibility: people stayed in their village, social class and jobs from birth to death, and they were vulnerably exposed to random events such as disease, famine or war. As causalities were not understood, it was not clear why or when things happened. Pregnancy, storms and love were mysterious events unrelated to causes we could see and understand. (Love still is.) Thinking about the future was therefore an entirely futile task for most of our ancestors.

This began to change in the seventeenth century. The discovery of the Americas; the Reformation; the French Revolution; the Enlightenment; and—of course—the Scientific Revolution made the future a space accessible to innovation, imagination and ideas. It is no coincidence that science fiction and political utopias were born at this time, but that was just the beginning. From the nineteenth century onwards, the progress made in healthcare and data collection meant personal futures became longer and more predictable: the concept of life expectancy was born. Thanks to data collection, humans also made progress in predicting the most unpredictable aspect of all—the weather. The even greater number of data allowed them to develop the most used system today to share the burden of a possibly dark future: insurances. At the same time, the future began to timidly emerge as a subject in philosophy, and physics took an increasing interest in time as such. The future also emerged in other fields: economic forecasts became standard governmental procedures, and the discovery of the role of genes in human health and behaviour led to sometimes wild ideas on how much could be predicted about personal fates.

However, it was not until the 1980s, when neurology developed brain imagery, that the tool allowed us to discover and understand what the future is to the human mind: in brain scans, it is almost as real as the past and the present. Proof now exists that the future isn't some distant time but what humans think, feel and do about it today. Studies have proven how much humans think about the future (a lot), how far forward they travel when doing so (not very), and shown that this activity increases well-being. Studies have even shown that the more a future is imagined, the likelier it is to happen. This isn't (just) pop psychology: the brain, once 'locked' onto a future target, will filter anything else out on the way there. Perhaps, most importantly, whether we are thinking about the daily future or that of the planet shows no difference in the brain: humans are capable of either if they direct their attention to it, although most people are not even aware of this.

The future in crisis

The final reason that most people rarely venture into the distant future is a more current one. At the moment, Western societies face two problems that make the future an undesirable time travel destination: the negative future(s) are multiple, and the previously positive future is no longer aspirational. In an ideal state, negative and positive futures hold each other in balance, but with one overwhelmingly dominant and the other glaringly absent, this leads to a negative total.

The negative futures are well known: climate change if left unchecked; the possible effects of artificial intelligence and robotics; the fast-changing norms and values of society; the possibility of a nuclear war; demographic decline; biodiversity loss; rising obesity; and future pandemics are just a few to name. These futures are not only negative, but they are also existential or even apocalyptic, threatening to irreversibly alter how humans live and work, and they affect a large number of people. Most importantly, they are often framed and viewed as something beyond human control. It is this perception of uncontrollability that closes the possibility space that the future normally is—at least temporarily. It also is not dissimilar to the ancient vision of the future as something humans do not control. In psychology, this is called the Cassandra Complex, whereby, in the face of excessive negativity, the human mind disengages.[3] In other words, just like the Trojans ignoring the mythological figure Cassandra who could see a trap laid by the Greeks, humans freeze in the face of too much bad news. Instead of acting, deciding, imagining and influencing the future, they fall into paralysis and do nothing, effectively abandoning the future.

This is already bad enough in itself, but it is not all. In previous instances of negative futures, a positive counter-future could balance things out, but Western society currently lacks this. The positive future to move towards that once existed is now a void.

For most of Europe, the aspirational future of the last seventy years was prosperity and freedom, with an evangelical desire to spread this future to the rest of the world based on the philosophy of progress that humanity was destined to improve its condition with every generation. Personal futures were anchored into this future: owning property and providing economic opportunity to children and grandchildren were cornerstones of the time ahead. In surveys, the question 'do you believe that your children will be financially better off than you?' was perhaps the only way that satisfaction with the future was measured. This future was rather successful all things considered: once the main rival for the future, the Soviet Union, dropped out

INTRODUCTION

of the race in 1991, the hunt for a different future (and with it, history as an evolutionary process towards something better) was over. By the early 2000s, more than half of the states in the world were democratic—up from 16% in 1950—and even more ran on capitalist economies.[4]

However, this future is in crisis. After marching onwards for decades, democracy has stopped expanding as a model in the world. Not only has it apparently lost appeal elsewhere, but in states that are already democratic, dissatisfaction is high—especially in the Anglosphere. Since 2005, dissatisfaction with democracy has doubled to 50% in the United States, the United Kingdom, Canada, New Zealand and Australia.[5] Similar numbers can be found in other democracies. There are many reasons why democracy is in crisis, but one of them is related to how democracy handles the future. Due to its short election cycles, it is accused of short-termism that renders it incapable of managing challenges that are further away.

Capitalism, the other main feature of our old future, is also facing criticism. In surveys, 52% of people agree that 'capitalism is doing more harm than good,'[6] amongst other things, because it is seen as the main culprit for climate change and has not entirely delivered on the promise of prosperity for all. The dissatisfaction with both democracy and capitalism might be unfair—both have delivered on many other fronts, making life today infinitely better than that of our ancestors—but their failure is seen less in their past and more in their future performance: what promises can both systems make that people aspire to today?

Given the twin challenge of negative futures and a void in a counter-future, it is perhaps not surprising that people are deeply unhappy about the future. In the United States, between half and two thirds of the population are said to be pessimistic about the future of almost anything—moral and ethical standards, education and racial equality.[7] Younger people especially are afraid of what is to come.[8] They are not alone in this: in various surveys, Europeans—especially Germans, French and Italians—and the Japanese generally are pessimistic about their personal future, the future of their country or that of the planet.[9] In this environment, fearmongering is a lucrative business, leading scientists such as astronomer Martin Rees to give out unscientific odds that, in his opinion, humanity has a 50% survival rate in the next 100 years.[10]

As a result, many give in to the Cassandra Complex and disengage entirely from the future.

Other futures on offer

Here is a hitch, though: this attitude seems to be a Western problem. In fact, surveys show that doom and gloom about the future seems to be a rich people's problem.

All over the world, people are optimistic that their children will be better off, that their country is going in the right direction, even that they can tackle climate change. Numbers are especially high amongst younger people—just not in the West.

One could argue that optimism is the result of the possibility space: precisely where people are less well off, room for improvement is possible. Nevertheless, while wealth does not guarantee optimism, it also does not stand in its way, as in the cases of China and Saudi Arabia, both of which regularly have 80% and 75% optimism rates in surveys and have levels of income comparable to Europe.[11] What they have in common are governments that have made the distant future positive cornerstones of their policies: China has promised to make the country 'stand tall in the world' by 2049, and Saudi Arabia's Vision 2030 is not only promising blooming cities in the desert but also a healthier and happier population.

In contrast, Western futures are not formulated in a positive way. Instead, they tend to focus on negatives, and a mindset of if you do not do such an action, things will get worse: limiting global warming to 1.5°C and keeping unemployment down and migrants out. The stories of the American and European futures are ones of status quo or returning to the past, promising to make things 'great again'. Of course, most democratic governments would not dream of promising to deliver by 2030—let alone 2050—when they will no longer be in power. However, by definition, the future is—and has to be—different from the present in order to enthuse people. Science fiction films are compelling precisely because they show us something that is different—ideally, better—from the now. No film portraying a society that successfully managed to keep things exactly the same would be a success. How a future is told is therefore as important as its contents, if not more. A story of decline, decrease or even continuity will always be less stimulating than one of growth, innovation, possibility and novelty.

This also explains why optimism rates in Russia have jumped from 40% to 52% since it invaded Ukraine, and rates of sadness and depression have decreased from 41% to 27%.[12] What the war did in this regard was re-open a possibility space that many Russians felt had been closed off with the success of the Western future. In 2021, a Russian think tank report noted that 'the future has become irrelevant... Once the "end of history" phase is over and the still unpredictable future arrives... there is a future again. It is not predestined, and every one of us can contribute to shaping it.'[13] While the war has made the future considerably more difficult to plan for 51% of Russians, it has given many the feeling that it will also be shaped by their own actions.[14]

INTRODUCTION

What does this mean?

Three elements can be deduced from this for the European future in crisis. First, pessimism or optimism about the future have less to do with how much disaster or wealth we expect in it and more to do with how much influence we have over said future. The more influence we think we have, the more optimistic we are. Influence, in turn, isn't an objective fact: it is a perception directly resulting from the number of options for the future we have come up with. This means that one of the ways to increase optimism is to formulate ways in which this future can be influenced and how different futures could be created, thereby identifying one's own room for manoeuvring.

Second, this is a job for both governments and citizens, but the former must lead the way. They not only have to give the distant future more space in their programmes by having more strategic foresight, but they also must tell a good story about the future, one that does not merely promise to maintain the status quo. Citizens will thank them for it: in surveys, people everywhere want their governments to think more long-term.[15] A shift in this direction has already occurred, with ideas ranging from appointing ministers (Sweden, United Arab Emirates), commissioners (European Union, Wales) or committees (Finland, United Nations) to represent the voices of future generations, legally enshrining their rights.

However, governments alone do not make the future. It is the ideas and attitudes of companies as well as individuals that shape it. Without a future-oriented movement, societies do not produce innovative ideas in technology, education or science fiction; they do not challenge the present, and they stop coming up with options for what the future could be. In some places, this movement is already well underway: the Long Now Foundation in California promotes the idea of conceiving of ourselves not as beings influencing the next 100 years but the next 10,000. In Japan, the Future Design movement has pioneered a unique form of citizens' assembly where some members had to represent residents from the future, and tech giant Soft Bank has created a $100 billion Vision Fund allowing for a 300-year horizon in planning.

Thinking long-term isn't only a morally right thing to do—it also comes with benefits. The longer ahead a company thinks, the higher revenues and profits are over time.[16] What applies to companies also applies to individuals: studies have shown that people with a broader temporal understanding looked more long-term at stock market performance and as a result made better financial decisions.[17] Just as capitalism is not doomed to short-termism, neither is democracy. The Intergenerational Solidarity Index measures how well states are doing in balancing the interests of different generations. While Iceland ranks first, the United

INTRODUCTION

Kingdom ranks at a meagre 45 and the United States at 62, the index also shows that democracies thinking long-term, rather than autocracies, are ultimately the best-suited political system for the future. This, together with the global optimism rates, shows that the philosophy of progress still has its supporters—just not so much where it originated—and, as such, is still valid. However, it requires undoing the effects of the Cassandra Complex to return to the possibility space that the future is.

The applied future

The practical format of a user's guide seems odd for a concept as abstract and philosophical as the future. However, this choice is a conscious one: the future is not some elitist phenomenon but the most human thing that exists. Every single human can imagine the future, be afraid of it and hope for it. It is also why this is not a strictly philosophical, psychological, physical, neurological, mathematical or historical book, but all of this and more. Precisely because the future is a horizontal phenomenon that runs through all things human, it cannot be explained by one or two disciplines alone. Moreover, as the future is structurally and phenomenologically the same at the personal or collective level, no distinction is made between those futures that are normally found in the self-help section and those restricted to the strategic foresight corner.

One can read this book as an individual trying to understand one's mind and life better, but one could equally read it as a company or government in need of more long-term thinking.

In either case, the structure of this book is designed to make the future as accessible and manageable as possible. Much like a user's guide for a vacuum cleaner, it comes with technical specifications in Chapter 1, addressing general aspects, including the future's purpose, types of futures, and where and when the future started. Chapter 2 lays out the different parts that make up the future, including the on-switch, present and past, as well as creativity. Operation instructions are found in Chapter 3, which explains the different steps of how to manage the future. Chapter 4 explains the safety instructions, including the risks of catastrophising, determinism, fake futures and wishful thinking. Should the future not work, Chapter 5 has all the troubleshooting, such as what to do when the future cannot be seen or is negative; how to handle the unexpected; and how to deal with the uninspired future. Lastly, as with every manual, the book ends with a warranty: not a promise that the future will be bright but that it always will be a possibility space.

In truth, we don't live in an unprecedentedly scary and unpredictable world, despite all the narratives saying otherwise. We live in a privileged time where being born gives someone a high certainty to live until old age and

INTRODUCTION

where one's future comes with substantial freedom in what to fill it with. Thanks to unimaginable progress, humans have emancipated themselves from a future that was outside their realm of influence 300 years ago to one they can anticipate, shape and dream up. Nevertheless, perhaps due to decades of certainty, entitlement and future laziness, the future now carries a sense of despair, of it not being predictable and of little knowledge on how to manoeuvre the possibility space that the future is.

These feelings are ultimately the reason I wrote this book. In my work as a strategic foresight advisor, I encountered two phenomena: the first was that people always wanted to know how to do it, how to think 'best' about the future, looking for a methodology or dataset that would give them the key to the kingdom of the future. They are often disappointed when they discover that the best way to think about the future is not as complicated as a methodology or as expensive as a dataset but much simpler: hone your mind. Being 'good' at the future means, first of all, being good at using one's own brain: being able to question one's beliefs and certainties, to seek out information that contradicts us, to manage one's emotions, to pay attention to novelty and to take our information from a variety of sources are all simple things; yet, many of us prefer not to do them. The trappings of the mind taught in school or university imply very little intellectual hygiene. Both people and governments are interested in the future, but both are a little lazy when it comes to actually doing the work. They would prefer to hire somebody to do it for them—which is why they end up falling prey to people selling false futures, often dressed up as catastrophism.

The second phenomenon is that I noticed people generally being chronically pessimistic, all the time, about pretty much anything, almost as if pessimism was a badge of intellectual honour. Even when shown the evidence of their past or present pessimism having been wrong, they were incapable of changing their mind. While this means they are not likely to excel at strategic foresight, it is also problematic in other ways as pessimism does not lead anywhere but to a sense of despair. (Overoptimism does not either, and an entire chapter in this book is dedicated to this topic.) The trick is to find the sweet spot where creativity, knowledge, wisdom, imagination and facts come together to outline the possibility space that the future is, imagine the best, prepare for the worst and live with surprise.

1

TECHNICAL SPECIFICATIONS

At first sight, the future is a simple thing: we all have it, it is not here yet, and if you believe some people, it has never been as unpredictable as it is now.

However, if you look a bit closer, you will discover that the future is everything but simple: we might all be able to imagine it, and some of us have the talent to do this more than others. Some of us think it is ahead of us in space; some think it makes much more sense to say it is behind us (because we cannot see it).[1] Some animals seem to have no sense of the future, but others, such as scrub jays, do.[2] For some, it is the stuff of fantastic films and series; for others, the time they never want to think about. Then, what do we know about this fascinating, complex thing? In this chapter, we examine the main features of the future, its purpose, the different types (yes, more than one) and how long it has existed.

THE FUTURE

1.1 *Characteristics*

The future is the process of imagining it.

Let us begin with the basics: the future is a time. Whilst its siblings, the past and the present, are times of things gone by and things happening now, the future is a time about things to come. Easy so far.

However, what is time, and what do we need to know about it in order to understand the future? The first thing is that time is relative, meaning that how it is perceived can differ considerably from person to person. This idea is a comparatively new one: for the longest time (no pun intended), humans thought that time was absolute—a phenomenon existing independently from us, much like flowers or the sun. They did notice, of course, that time perception often differed from the clocks that measured it, but they were not sure how to explain it. Therefore, time—and with it the future—played almost no role in how humans conceived of themselves and their existence, and little ancient philosophical reflection on it is available.[3] This began to change with the Enlightenment, when philosophers such as Immanuel Kant began to ponder the question of whether time was actually real. His colleague J. M. E. McTaggart was so convinced that he even proposed to get rid of all tenses. (This idea never gained much traction in English, but the fact that not all languages have tenses in the same way that European languages

TECHNICAL SPECIFICATIONS

do—some have no tenses at all, and some even have two tenses for the future—supports the idea that time is indeed a matter of perception rather than absolute.)[4]

Today, thanks to the likes of Swiss physicist Albert Einstein, we know that time is an experience humans share but also that it expands and contracts depending on context and person.[5] Not only is time individually perceived differently, but physicists are now convinced that the direction of its flow is just a (powerful) human illusion. In reality, time has no clear succession of past, present and future—they all coexist in equal measure.[6] (Which means theories of time travel and alternate universes are no longer mere science fiction fantasies.) Within this illusion, there are only two statements on which everybody agrees: time is perceived as flowing in one direction, just like an arrow (from the past to the future), and time is a continuum—it does not stop and re-start.

This means that 'the future' does not exist as an objective, observable phenomenon: it is an individual, unique perception taking place entirely in one's head, just as the present and the past. It also means that it is as real as the other two.

This might sound odd at first: for most of us, the future is the least 'real' of the three times we have. After all, we can experience the present with our senses, and we have plenty of evidence of the past: our own memory of course, but also tangible things such as books, buildings, art and stories of people that lived then. It is because of this that we accept commonly taught retrodiction, the definitive story of things past, as historical reality. In contrast to the past or present, we seem to have no evidence of the future. We cannot touch it, smell it or ask people who live there what it will be like. As a result, a common misconception of the future is that it is a time that is yet to come and therefore not real, and what is not real cannot be measured, conceptualised or shared.

Except this is wrong.

Is the future real?

All time perceptions—the future included—are generated in several different parts of the brain. This is what makes time different from other senses such as hearing or feeling, which have only one specific sensory system in the brain. (Don't confuse this with the body clock or circadian rhythm regulating our hormones and energy levels—it is almost entirely disconnected from this and runs practically like Swiss clockwork for just a little over 24 hours.) Therefore, we don't have only one clock but several—hidden away in our brain—that measure and project time into the past and future.

These clocks keep what we call subjective time, which can be substantially out of sync with clock time. Whether you are on a fantastic holiday that went by much quicker than the average week at work or are impatiently waiting for a train, time seems to be as elastic as a piece of chewing gum. Don't worry, there is nothing wrong: it just shows how individual time actually is. How we perceive it depends on what we do, where we are and who we are with, but also how we feel physically: when we are cold, we perceive time to run faster, whereas when we are hot (or just had a cheeseburger, really!) time runs slower.[7] Emotions, too, have an impact on time perception: fear, for instance, makes it run much slower, almost as if the brain had the capacity to extend time in order to find a solution to the problem.[8] This sense of subjective time is not only about how fast or slow time seems to move but also a feeling for temporal distance: how far into the future or past that things are in relation to us.[9] These mind clocks serve as a temporal GPS, to help us feel where we are in time and how far away we are from things that have happened and things that will happen.

The future is generated particularly in three areas in the brain: the frontal lobe, parietal lobe and medial temporal lobe. What is interesting about these three lobes is that they are not only in charge of creating the future together, but they also have other jobs that give us some ideas on what the purpose of future generation actually is. The frontal lobe, for instance, is responsible for working memory, decision making and problem solving, and makes sure that memories are not confused with the present; this could indicate that the purpose of the future is to make decisions, often using memory as a database. The parietal lobe oversees processing sensory signals from the body and orientation, turns letters into words and words into thoughts and has a navigational function, which indicates that time relates to space—it is no coincidence that we often use spatial words to describe time—but also to stories. Lastly, the medial temporal lobe includes the hippocampus and regulates memory, learning, emotion and language—all of which are crucial for human reasoning.[10]

When we compare the future to the past in brain scans, we find that we might have clearer mental images when it comes to the past, but we have more emotions when we think about the future. Moreover, the further we travel into the future, the more active the hippocampus becomes (the area responsible for emotion, memory and learning). This means that we can not only recall the taste or smell of a Madeleine—which inspired Proust's seven-volume novel *A la recherche du temps perdu*—but we can even imagine what the first cocktail on our holiday will taste like, even if we have never had a cocktail![11] This puts a dent in the present's claim of being the only 'real' time. Not only can we literally feel the future's outline, but we have a clear idea of how far away it is from where we are today.[12] To our brains, the future is therefore almost as real as the past or present.

TECHNICAL SPECIFICATIONS

The time machine

This capacity is called mental time travel: the creative process of imagining in detail what a future occurrence can look and feel like way before it has materialised. In science fiction, travelling to the future always involves some type of machine. Most of us have heard of the 1895 book *The Time Machine* by H. G. Wells, although he was not the first to imagine time travel. Spanish writer Enrique Gaspar was the first to come up with it in *El anacronópete* (literally 'the one who flies against time') in 1887.

In reality, we don't need a machine: all we need is our mind. Imagining a time that has never been sounds like an exceptional superpower, but we use this skill pretty much daily. The average human thinks about the future 59 times a day, or once every 16 minutes; in total, one spends three times as much time thinking about what is coming next as one thinks about the past; and when one thinks about the past, half the time it is to reflect on its implications for the future.[13]

Whether we do it intentionally—for instance, when we're making plans—or unintentionally—when our mind wanders—imagining the future is fundamentally different from knowing (or believing) what will happen next: it is an individual, creative, imaginary and sensorial process in which a hologram of a future reality is produced, not dissimilar to the Holodeck in Star Trek.[14] It is this capacity that serves as the basis of main human attributes such as expectation, choice, decision, preference and free will. For this reason, some believe that we are not Homo sapiens at all, but Homo prospectus: a being defined not by its capacity to reason but by that to mentally travel to the future.[15] It is not a coincidence that Greek mythology portrays Prometheus ('foresight') as a hero that frees humanity by bringing it fire and the arts, whereas his brother Epimetheus ('hindsight') is not only mostly forgotten but often portrayed as a bit of a fool. What this pair's story is trying to convey is that the future—and having a sense of it—is crucial for humanity.

1.2 Intended use: What is the future for?

The purpose of the future is to make the best possible choice under conditions of uncertainty; it also creates a sense of control, serves as a motor for growth and makes us happy.

This seems obvious when imagining what it would be like not to have one: from spending all our money, to doing damage to our bodies, to being reckless with our personal relationships and belongings, we would do a lot of things that our future self would regret. However, when we look closer, we find that the capacity to imagine both the worst to avoid and the best ahead (and everything in between) is about more than just damage control.

TECHNICAL SPECIFICATIONS

First, having a sense of the future is crucial for learning, which itself is linked to survival. After all, what would be the purpose of having experiences one remembers if not to learn from them for the future? Do not cross the road again when the sign is red, or you might be run over as almost happened the other day; do not hang out by the water hole alone, or the tiger might come darting for you as it did for your antelope friend the other day. No matter whether this applies to the distant past or the twenty-first century, memories are there to learn from, and to improve one's survival chances in the future.

Nevertheless, this is only the most basic function of the future, which has more sophisticated purposes. To understand them, we need to consider one of the main features of the future: uncertainty. Although we may say many things with certainty about the future, we cannot be sure about many more, and this is something humans hate—so much so that they even prefer bad news over an uncertainty that could lead to good news.[16] Of course, not every level of uncertainty is equal: some are more ambiguous than others.

Regardless of how extensive uncertainty is, however, the only tool we have to deal with it is our capacity to imagine different futures. By thinking through different scenarios, we reduce uncertainty as we map out possibilities, reflect on probabilities and identify avenues for action. Together, this reduces uncertainty, gives us a feeling (or an illusion) of control and security and—perhaps most importantly—also makes it a lot easier for us to make decisions.[17]

This is why we can say that after survival, the purpose of generating the future is to make decisions and act on them. We think that this is because time—and with it, action—only goes forward (or at least that is what we perceive it to be). The only time that you can influence with your action is therefore the future (even though you can change how you think about the past, but that is another story). Being able to decide and act would therefore be an important talent to have as a human.

The future as philosophy

That is: if you subscribe, at least to some extent, to the notion of free will. Since Aristotle—and until today—the debate has raged amongst philosophers and theologians alike on how much influence humans have on their own future. Adherents of fatalism will say none: the future is fixed and cannot be changed, no matter what humans do. In this logic, life is like a film: you might not know how it will end, and this is predetermined from the outset whether you throw popcorn at the screen or not. A second school of thought, determinism, equally believes that the future is fixed but human action is an integral part of it. In this logic, you will have an illusion of choice, and it is this choice that will set the future in motion. An episode of the Netflix series *Black Mirror*, 'Bandersnatch', captures this idea when the viewer is prompted to decide the main character's choices. (If you watch the episode repeatedly, you will realise that the ending is always the same.) However, scientifically speaking, we have no proof that either fatalists or determinists are right: although neurology has spotted brain activity that precedes a decision, it is believed that this activity means the brain is readying itself by creating options, rather than it being an indication of free will being an illusion.[18]

Lastly, supporters of free will say that neither fatalists nor determinists are right: humans might make confusing decisions at times, but they are their own; therefore, they bear the responsibility for the future they create. A whole section of philosophy called existentialism emerged from the mid-nineteenth century onwards, reflecting these ideas: it is the only school of thought to have an extensive understanding of what the future means to being human. Representatives include Søren Kierkegaard (*The Concept of Anxiety*, 1844), Martin Heidegger (*Being and Time*, 1927), Jean-Paul Sartre (*Being and Nothingness*, 1943) and Hannah Arendt (*Between Past and Future*, 1961), amongst others.

That this school has emerged only after we started thinking of time as something that is individually created rather than absolute is perhaps no coincidence. After all, does the very capacity to think about the future not prove that it exists to create many different possible ones?[19] If we look at it that way, we can see that the purpose of the future is not only to survive and feel more secure in uncertainty but also to create options from which we can choose,[20] and the more options we have, the more freedom we have to choose. To push the idea further: the more futures one can imagine, the freer one is.

This may also explain why we actually enjoy thinking about the future as a space for possibility.[21] We prefer Fridays—for we have a pleasant future coming right after them—over Sundays, even though we work on one but not the other.[22] In other words, we prefer a pleasant future over a pleasant present. Studies have shown that we prefer thinking about something nice that we think might happen over something nice that actually happened: in the direct competition between actual positive past and potential positive future events, the future wins.[23]

Why is that? In large part, this is because we constantly overestimate the good that lies ahead for us personally. Most people, you and I included, have an unspoken expectation that the next holiday will be great, the next date could be the one, and the next job could lead to a great career. We like imagining our future because we are biased to think it will be good. This seems to be a near-universal human trait: whether nine-year old schoolchildren[24] or adults as old as 80,[25] people all believe that good things lie in store for them—regardless of race, gender and socioeconomic status.[26] The further in the future things are, the more optimistic we are,[27] and in surveys, people agree that this is a good trait to have.[28]

This human penchant to enjoy thinking about the future might seem a bit odd. After all, as a species we have developed an innate understanding of our own mortality; thus, our personal future has a defined endpoint. This insight alone would make the capacity to prospect (i.e. to imagine alternatives stretching into the future) quite a debilitating one. One would see disease, decay and death. However, our brain has developed not one but several mechanisms to cope with this insight: first, none of us really grasp our own death as an inevitable reality. Sure, we know on some level—but as one study showed, our brain literally reaches a dead end when conceiving its own nothingness.[29] Second, the optimism bias overrules all the negative things that the future could hold for us so that we can continue to indulge in 'futuring'. It is as if the very knowledge of death had to be born at the same as its denial for us to be able to live with it.[30] Without it, we would perceive the future accurately as a mixed bag of positive and negative things; we might become anxious and defeatist and stop striving, evolving and aiming for better outcomes. Lastly, some scientists believe that the purpose of the future is to create our sense of self. Just like memories, ideas of what we want (or don't want) to happen are ingredients that shape our identity.[31]

1.3 Typologies: Types of futures

Futures differ in two ways: How far away they are and how much influence we have over them.

Although we use the term 'future' in the single form, the types of future are various. As we have seen, the future is a time, and just as time distances are different, futures are different depending on distance. As we have also learnt, however, the future's purpose is to do something with it; thus, the futures are different depending on how much influence we have over them. The two criteria we use to categorise futures are distance and influence.[32] These give rise to four futures that are related to each other like Russian dolls: the daily future is part of our lifetime, which is part of our era, which is part of a longer-term future.

The first is the future of routine, which we call daily future—what I will eat tomorrow, when I will pick up my children from school, when I will meet my friend for dinner. This type of future is mostly cyclical: it is a repetition of similar actions with the same objective. Due to its cyclical character, most of us would not even call it a future, but it is one. If we wanted to measure this future, we would give it days or weeks, perhaps months at the most. This is the one we think about the most because we determine it with actions and see almost immediate results.

The second future is the future of our lifetime. Here, we allot typical questions, such as when and where we will start working, get married, have a career breakthrough, publish a book, have children and so forth. It is normally conceived of in years depending on how old one is. This future is linear rather than cyclical: it flows along our chronological age and normally has a human lifespan of about 100 years. That is why it is also finite (whereas the daily future often seems eternal thanks to its repetitive nature). This future has different chapters, like a book, and is heavily influenced by what society thinks it should be.[33] Society's ideas for our future are concentrated in our 20s and 30s, which is why many of us run out of ideas for the future when we hit 40 and begin to think about our legacy (i.e. our future beyond our death, a phenomenon called the midlife crisis).[34] (More on this and how to handle it in Chapter 5). Somewhat paradoxically, we get better at imagining and feeling our personal futures as we get older as the capacity to generate the future depends on how much memory we have.[35] It is also for this reason that older adults continue to have vivid ideas of the future even if, objectively, they might not have much time left.[36] It may not be surprising to hear that teenagers think less about their personal future than middle-aged adults; this is not because they have so much of it, but rather, they lack the relevant data to imagine it.[37]

What both futures have in common is that they are—or at least appear to be—under one's control. You have agency to fill these futures with your actions.

Perhaps this is why you feel notoriously optimistic about this type of future. You are convinced that the next date, holiday or job will be pretty good (you might be wrong, but that will not stop you from being biased next time).[38]

However, you have little or no control over two more types of future influencing you.

Our collective futures

The first of these two futures is the future of our time (also called epoch or era). We give these eras names, but we often do this afterwards, not while we are in them. Eras are separated by a host of trends that culminate in an event symbolising the change, and they can be anywhere between 10 and 30 years long. Older examples include eras defined by the lifetime of a monarch ('The Victorian Era'), but more recent ones are defined by technological innovation of that time ('The digital era'). In many other cases, it is left to historians to tell us when a new time has begun.[39] Most companies will situate themselves in this future: while they do manage daily futures, most of them will set targets for themselves anywhere between 1 and 10 years in the future.

This future is a collective one as it is influenced by many, and it creates the backdrop for all our personal futures.[40] The problem with this future is that we have little influence over it—less than over our personal futures, and even less than over our daily futures. When this future seems to go well, we can sit back and relax;

when it does not, this not only means that our own future is in trouble, but we cannot even do something about it—a bit like sitting in the back of a car with an awful driver at the wheel.

It is especially common for people to feel pessimistic about this type of future while at the same time being more optimistic about one's own future. There are two reasons for this: the first is the aforementioned optimism bias we have when it comes to our own future, and the second is that we feel generally more optimistic about something when we can influence it.[41] (Perhaps best embodied in American positivism.)[42] Cultures and countries differ in their degrees of optimism, pessimism and influence when it comes to their personal and their collective futures, but the trend—optimistic at home, pessimistic elsewhere—is pretty much the same everywhere in Europe and the United States.

Last, a fourth future is what we call sacral future. It spans way beyond us and the times in which we live. This future has two characteristics: first, like the future of our personal lives, it has an endpoint, even though this is not dated; second, it is normally flanked with a notion of human responsibility. Perhaps the most prominent example is Judgement Day in Christianity and Islam, the day on which humans will be judged for their actions (hence implying at least some extent of free will—why would one be held accountable for actions one did not choose?). Despite regular claims by groups that the end is near, neither religion has given a date for when this will occur. Other examples that can be included in this type of future are the fate of the planet, either because of climate change and biodiversity loss or because of a nuclear holocaust.[43] These types of sacral futures differ from the religious ones in that human responsibility is collective rather than individual, but what they have in common is that they ask existential questions about humanity's purpose.

On the frequency of each future

We switch back and forth between these four different futures like we change gears in a car. However, just as an urban dweller will not often be in fifth gear, a regular person will not spend much time in the sacral future. The fact is that the further away a future is and the less influence we have over it, the less we will think about it. According to one American survey, the coming month is the future most commonly thought about, followed by the coming year. From there on, mind travellers become fewer: once or twice a month, 22% think about the future three or five years from now; more than half almost never think about a future 10 years away, and three quarters do not think of a future 30 years away.[44] This means that while we all have the capacity to imagine futures far away, most of us never think much further than the coming year.

TECHNICAL SPECIFICATIONS

In part, this is because our capacity to feel the distance to a certain future decreases the farther we go. This is because our perception of time gets increasingly out of sync as we lose external cues for passing time.

Think of it this way: you know when a day has passed because the sun rises again. You also know when a month has passed because you might be a moon watcher or because you menstruate. The seasons also affect this perception: when spring comes around again, you know—you feel—that a year has passed. It is perhaps for this reason that agriculture is often credited with giving humans a sense of time. (Although, as we will see later, about 10,000 years passed between the beginnings of agriculture and the first calendar; thus, it was not just agriculture that created a sense of time.) Days, months and about one year are therefore levels of future you will find easy to feel in terms of distance as the environment gives us visible cues. (If you are wondering about the week, the seven days were not taken from external cues but chosen by the Babylonians in the fourth century BC as they had to cut up the moon cycle into manageable chunks.) Beyond the year, external time cues are few and far between; therefore, the next visible indication of time passing is life itself. (Which is perhaps also why we have a limited vocabulary to describe the future: tomorrow, next week, next month and next year is all we have.) Perhaps this is why most of us imagine the future to be at the maximum 100 years away—about a human lifetime.[45] Calendars and watches are no substitute for this feeling: they are the crutch that help us sync it with how the rest of society feels time when we have gone off into our own time perception world, but they cannot themselves generate that feeling.

This means that we generally struggle when it comes to really long distances such as decades or, trickier still, centuries or even millennia. It is perhaps also why participants in a study chose to travel much farther into the past (157 years) than into the future (40 years): they can imagine the past based on information received from others, but the future must be filled entirely with their imagination.

The other reason for why we don't travel to the far future that often is that we lose a sense of a continuous self the farther we go. This is essentially being able to feel who you were five minutes ago, who you are now and who you will be in the future. This sense of self becomes increasingly weaker the farther you go into the future, and at some point, your brain will literally imagine your future self as if it were somebody else. It is unclear why this is the case, but it can have troubling consequences: if your future self is somebody else, you can take out loans on their health, finances or emotional lives. After all, it will not be you who is paying the price. (This also explains why humans do not exactly excel at prevention: from smoking to sunscreen and seatbelts, it is hard work to convince humans of things of which they will not see immediate effects. More on this in the next chapter.)[46]

This does not mean that our futures are year-long only, but it does mean that the quality of the near-future and the distant future that we imagine will differ, and we have to think harder about it. Once we time travel without a natural sense of time passing, we will be increasingly out of sync with actual time. This means that our futures might be accurate in terms of what will happen but not when it comes to the exact timing. Once we think about the future without a clear sense of self, we are biased towards the present: we underestimate change because we tend to believe everything will more or less remain the same. One study for instance showed that people continuously underestimated how much they would change over a decade.[47]

Lastly, we suspect that our accelerated sense of time plays a role in us mentally spending more time in the near than in the distant future. This isn't so much because time is actually moving faster—it is not—but because more things are happening within this time. As a result, our attention is locked into here.[48] (The fact that we spend less time daydreaming and more doomscrolling also leaves little space to think about the distant future.) To find out where you sit in your predisposed time orientation, take this test below.

THE FUTURE

Table: Consideration of Future Consequences Scale

	Not at all like me					Very much like me
1. I consider how things might be in the future, and try to influence those things with my day-to-day behavior.	1	2	3	4	5	6	7
2. Often I engage in a particular behavior in order to achieve outcomes that may not result for many years.	1	2	3	4	5	6	7
3. I only act to satisfy immediate concerns, figuring the future will take care of itself.	7	6	5	4	3	2	1
4. My behavior is only influenced by the immediate (i.e., a matter of days or weeks) outcomes of my actions.	7	6	5	4	3	2	1

TECHNICAL SPECIFICATIONS

		Not at all like me					Very much like me
5.	My convenience is a big factor in the decisions I make or the actions I take.	7	6	5	4	3	2	1
6.	I am willing to sacrifice my immediate happiness or wellbeing in order to achieve future outcomes.	1	2	3	4	5	6	7
7.	I think it is important to take warnings about negative outcomes seriously even if the negative outcome will not occur for many years.	1	2	3	4	5	6	7
8.	I think it is more important to perform a behavior with important distant consequences than a behavior with less important immediate consequences.	1	2	3	4	5	6	7

THE FUTURE

	Not at all like me						Very much like me
9. I generally ignore warnings about possible future problems because I think the problems will be resolved before they reach crisis level.	7	6	5	4	3	2	1
10. I think that sacrificing now is usually unnecessary since future outcomes can be dealt with at a later time.	7	6	5	4	3	2	1
11. I only act to satisfy immediate concerns, figuring that I will take care of future problems that may occur at a later date.	7	6	5	4	3	2	1
12. Since my day-to-day work has specific outcomes, it is more	7	6	5	4	3	2	1

TECHNICAL SPECIFICATIONS

	Not at all like me						Very much like me
important to me than behavior that has distant outcomes.							
13. When I make a decision, I think about how it might affect me in the future.	1	2	3	4	5	6	7
14. My behavior is generally influenced by future consequences.	1	2	3	4	5	6	7

Source: Science of Behaviour Change, "Consideration of Future Consequences Scale".

77–98 Points "Future Assurance"

As far as the future is concerned, it's not just about foresight for you, but also about play and fun. You weigh risks and chances of winning and losing, but ultimately the future is a game you enjoy playing.

55–76 Points "Equilibrium of Times"
You have the equilibrium between times figured out quite well: you often think about the future and consider your decisions, but you live very much in the now and understand how to balance the dance between times. A small dose of present is just as important—your future self will thank you.

33–54 Points "The Short Future Stretch"
Your future stretch is not particularly long. You think regularly about the next vacation or the next dinner, but rather seldom about the next year, let alone the next decade. Let's think big—your future self will thank you for it.

14–32 Points "Future Amnesia"
Future? Which future? This result means that the present principle is taken somewhat too seriously, too much in the here and now and now and now. This is usually a lot of fun, but the future will have to foot the bill. If the present absorbs you too much, create moments for yourself where you consciously make decisions for the future.

1.4 Origins: The history of the future

The future is considered so human it is almost eternal: it was always there, and it always will be. Except this is not entirely true. Think of your own childhood: if you have extraordinarily good memory, you will recall a time when you personally had no future: before we are three or four years old, we have no conception of words such as 'yesterday' or 'tomorrow', and we permanently live in the now. The future sets in for us as individuals when we outgrow the early amnesia children have and begin to have memories. Once we can remember things we experienced, we equally begin to understand that things will come, although, at the age of four, our perception of the future is not fine-tuned, and we barely grasp the idea of next week. A real sense of temporal distance—say, three weeks to Christmas—does not develop before the age of seven.[49] In other words: your future grows along with you. The older you get, the further into the future you can see.

Just as human individuals have different senses of the future at different stages of their lives, so did humanity as a whole.

We have only little evidence of our distant ancestors having a fully developed sense of the future. From burial sites found all over the world, we can guess that they had an understanding of death—by definition, a future event—but also an afterlife, as shown by the offerings and items found in these sites. The tools and paint they left behind also are indications that they could plan and innovate, both of which are ingredients of foresight. However, we have no other evidence of a sense of the future or of how they perceived time passing.[50]

THE FUTURE

The first direct evidence we have for a sense of the future dates to 2400 BC, when the Sumer civilisation in Mesopotamia created the first calendar. This calendar was not wildly dissimilar to ours: it was divided into 12 months of 29–30 days each, and although it had no weeks, it had planned days off on the 1st, 7th and 15th of each month. This structure was based on observations of their planetary environment: days would be counted from sunset to sunset, and months were based on the lunar cycle. Just like we do, the Sumer added an extra day every four years. The Sumer calendar also had wet and dry seasons, indicating that its purpose was to help people prepare for the different agricultural seasons. Without such a planning system, they would be surprised by the floods of the Euphrates and Tigris, but with it, they could maximise the benefits and reduce potentially negative effects.

What helped the Sumer come up with this first calendar was the fact that not only had they developed writing, but they also used it to record important events along with star constellations serving as dates. As we have seen earlier, history and experience help us pass on lessons for the future. The Sumer also tried to match these events with preceding signs to predict the future—a practice known as divination. Although they were convinced that their influence on future events was limited by the Gods, they sought to determine what they had planned for them and reduce uncertainty to some extent.

This involved a thorough observation of the environment, the stars, people's appearance as well as the entrails of animals, such as sheep. The interpretation of these signs was never random: the Sumer kept a close record of signs that occurred during previous events— say, a lion had appeared outside the city gate just before the fall of a ruler; thus, a lion appearing again indicated that trouble was in store for the ruler. This practice was called omen collection. Judging from the material the Sumer left behind, this was a frequent exercise.[51] Although the Sumer got causality wrong (the lion had nothing to do with a leader's demise), they were still the first to look for patterns in their environment to make the future less uncertain and to use the past as a tool to understand the future.

With the calendar, the star signs, the recording of events and even divination, the Sumer invented the future as a concept: they did not just know that there was a future, but they actively sought to manage it.

The first future (mis)managers

Both the calendar and divination as tools to manage the future spread from Mesopotamian civilisations: from ancient Egypt to the Babylonians, Assyrians, ancient Greeks and Romans to Persia and the Indus valley, humans used both to manage the time to come.[52] What is worth noting is that these tools also appeared in extremely distant places, such as in ancient China and in the Norte Chico, a region of what is now Peru.[53] This means that, once writing and star-gazing had been developed, humanity as a whole began to develop an understanding of the future as a time that can be managed and anticipated more or less at the same time.

Timeline of the first future managers

Who	What	When
Sumer	Calendar Divination	2400 BC
Babylonians	Horoscopes	700–500 BC
Ancient China	Oracle bone reading	1300 BC
Maya	Calendar	500 BC
Harappa (Pakistan)	Boards and dice	2000 BC
Ancient Greece	Oracles and seers	700 BC
Ancient Rome	Crystal ball	First century AD
India	Palm-reading	500 BC

These approaches to the future had two limits: firstly, future-gazing was reserved to the elites. This made sense insofar as that individuals in highly hierarchical societies had little influence over their own lives anyway. As we have seen, one's attitude to the future is always shaped by how much influence one has over it. Secondly, the Sumer future was not something one

TECHNICAL SPECIFICATIONS

could in any way change but only anticipate once one had read the omens right.

The Babylonians, a civilisation that succeeded the Sumer in Mesopotamia, innovated in both regards once they moved from mere stargazing and position-recording to calculating when a star would reappear. This was nothing short of revolutionary: it changed the way they saw their environment and, with it, the future, as no longer a random occurrence of events overseen by temperamental Gods but a repetition of predictable patterns. From observing the star movements, the Babylonians had moved to predicting their future positions.

Based on this insight, the Babylonians went overboard: they were now convinced that they could predict a whole range of things unrelated to the stars, such as the lives and personalities of people born under a certain star sign. You guessed it: the horoscope (literally 'the markers of the hour', meaning the hour of birth) was born around 500 BC.[54] Not only did the Babylonians turn the future into something that could be predicted with mathematical accuracy, but they also laid the basics for future management for individuals. While the horoscope was first reserved for the king and later the kingdom's elites, it quickly proliferated to other levels of society and, of course, to other countries and cultures.

THE FUTURE

In ancient Rome, divination was a tool to not only manage the future but manipulate it. Cicero was convinced that Caesar was guilty of that and even wrote a strongly worded treatise against it in 44 BC,[55] explaining at length why he thought that one was better off asking subject matter experts rather than oracles for what would happen. While he certainly had ulterior motives against Caesar, Cicero was also very much influenced by the Stoics, a group of thinkers convinced that every effect had a cause. This might sound obvious today, but it took humanity a long time to come around to this insight. For the longest time, effects were just considered the (sometimes random) acts of Gods or God.

In general, the future was, at this point, not something humans could do much about; fatalism and determinism were the dominant attitudes towards the time to come. It was also believed that there was no supreme reward for good behaviour in this life: almost all humans were believed to end up in the underworld (only a few chosen ones deemed particularly worthy would go to Elysium), and heaven was reserved for the Gods.

Enter the humans: The future as choice

This changed when first Hinduism and Buddhism and later Christianity and Islam (and to some extent Judaism) introduced a radical new idea: responsibility for one's actions beyond this life. While all major religions posited a more or less distant end to all things, they differed in terms of the holding of individual accountability. For Hinduism and Buddhism, actions in this life will determine the next life, resting on an idea of rebirth. In Christianity and Islam, humans will be placed in Heaven or Hell after death depending on how they behaved on Earth. In Judaism, the different currents have differed over time with regard to how much personal action will determine where one will end up after death.[56]

The main ingredient in personal responsibility is, of course, free will, and with it, human agency rooted in their understanding of the future. Now, humans had choices to make and would be held responsible for them in the future. The future was not something that could be known in advance precisely because it depended on human choice and action, and this was emphasised further by the prohibition on divination in Christianity and Islam. Of course, Christianity and Islam still posited that God, as the master of everything, created the future and the fate of individuals with it, but within that setting, personal responsibility was crucial.

By the Middle Ages, the Catholic Church had diluted the Christian concept of personal responsibility: it first introduced the concept of purgatory (a place between Heaven and Hell where humans can cancel out their sins by sitting through punishments) and later indulgences.

Now, one could literally pay to go to Heaven or make up for sins by enduring punishments in this life.

In came two preachers with different ideas about the future: Martin Luther was convinced that it was not deeds that would absolve a human being but faith alone—thereby cancelling out the possibility to make up for past sins through payment or punishment. Protestantism got rid of the confessional, thereby putting all responsibility on the individual for its actions. John Calvin, in turn, was convinced that, free will or not, humans are still predestined to a fate God chose for them regardless of what they do.[57] Somewhat in contrast to common perception, there are several different Protestant understandings of the future. What these understandings have in common is the rejection of the possibility to atone for one's sins in this life.

The discovery of the future

The turning point for all things related to the future arrived in the seventeenth century, when the future became no longer a time where God would judge humans but a time whose outline was the result of human action. Until then, science was no independent field, and the world was explained primarily through theology and philosophy. However, following Copernicus, Galileo and Kepler, physicists such as René Descartes and Isaac Newton were convinced that the world actually worked much like a machine—a

TECHNICAL SPECIFICATIONS

mechanic sequence of events in which each event causes the next one. Descartes, along with Scottish philosopher David Hume, rejected the causality of Aristotle and others, thereby laying the foundation for what we still believe today: every effect has a cause.[58] In his 1748 book *An Enquiry Concerning Human Understanding*, Hume even wrote that causation is the 'connecting principle that connects the past with the future'. All one now had to do was find these causes, and the world would be predictable. This was such a groundbreaking idea that philosophers considered themselves to be scientific revolutionaries. They found that the sun does not, actually, revolve around Earth and that gravity is the result of planetary motion, among many other things. While things started in astronomy, they quickly expanded to all other areas of human life, such as medicine, biology and the social sciences. The quest to understand everything then began and is still ongoing.

If every effect has a cause, God's ways are no longer mysterious, but the world can be understood—at least partly—and with it, future effects can also be understood. Suddenly, the future was to be primarily the result of human action. With this responsibility came bigger questions: if the time ahead is ours, where do we lead it? Is there a deeper meaning to it all, and is there any way of knowing what we should do?

2

THE FUNCTIONS OF EACH PART

The future is not one big blob: much like a vacuum cleaner, it is made up of different parts that interplay with each other. There are four parts: the power button; the present; the past; and our creativity. How big or small each part is and how they interact with each other will vary wildly from person to person, even if they use similar or even identical ingredients. That is because our future parts depend on ourselves: our age, our bodily senses, our culture, our personality, our history and experiences, our values, goals and even our current mood. Just like our fingerprints, the parts that make our future(s) are unique to us—whether we are individuals, companies, governments or entire countries.

2.1 *The power button*

There are two ways to switch on the future: a spontaneous method and a deliberate method.

THE FUTURE

Our mind has, in the temporal sense, three gears: past, present and future. While it can jump around between them, it is, at any given moment, only in one. Simply put, we cannot be in two places at the same time mentally: while we are focused on a task in front of us, say surfing a wave, we cannot simultaneously think about the future. As you will see below, futuring mostly happens when we are not focused on something else. However, to be in the future gear, we have to actively switch there.

Then, how do we do this? In two ways: we can direct our attention there on purpose, or we do it somewhat unconsciously, almost by accident. Whereas the former is planning and all its productive cousins, the latter is known as mind-wandering. Both have different purposes and will produce different futures; while some, such as governments and companies, will rely more on planning, individuals will tend to use more mind-wandering. However, as you will see below, the two are (or should be) complementary: you need to alternate between both switches to achieve optimum results.

Let us begin with mind-wandering. As the term suggests, this is a process whereby your mind jumps, like a monkey from tree to tree, from one thought to the next, weaving the jumps into a flowing stream of a story. We do this often: studies have shown that our mind is off doing its own thing for half of our waking hours, and the majority of its meanderings concern the future. We mostly use playful, wishful and constructive images

THE FUNCTIONS OF EACH PART

about things we need or want to do, unresolved desires (ranging from love interests to career goals or even revenge urges) and a whole range of other things that concern the future. Although it is not quite clear why the mind chooses to cycle through certain elements more than others, mind-wandering towards the future seems to mostly concern things that our mind thinks might require preparation in some form. For instance, we would normally not sit around and think extensively about how to spell Arizona the next time we are asked, but we can spend a lot of time worrying about giving a speech next week. One study showed that people who had been told that they would be quizzed on geography later on spent 70% of their subsequent mind-wandering thinking about geography—as opposed to 10% when they had not been told about the upcoming quiz.[1] Where your mind will wander depends, therefore, entirely on yourself: your tasks, your ambitions, your worries and your dreams. Letting it wander deliberately is a useful tool to get to know yourself better and perhaps move closer to the future you want. That the brain does this was a bit of a surprise to scientists, who thought, for the longest time, that a brain on standby does nothing but just sit there. Instead, the brain without a particular task wanders off to do its own thing. 'Being without a task' can mean many different things: literally doing nothing while waiting for something; being engaged in something that requires little cognitive effort, like driving a car or chopping tomatoes; or being bored while listening to a lecture.

The benefits of mind-wandering

Mind-wandering is effortless and spontaneous, and it can even be an enjoyable, relaxing experience. For instance, you could begin daydreaming about your next holiday, move to what dinners you will have there, then to what you will or could wear to dinner, then to what you should pack, and then remember that you are out of sunscreen. In all cases, the mind wanders off by itself: in other words, it is not a conscious decision. You cannot actively begin to mind-wander, but you can create the conditions for it. This is where the twenty-first century might make mind-wandering an endangered species: not only does our educational system make little space for subjects that encourage open-minded exploration such as the arts, music or literature, but social media and smartphones fill our mind's moments of rest with content that effectively sedates it.

This is a problem as mind-wandering has a useful purpose. Despite its undeservedly lazy image, mind-wandering is a goal-driven, value-based and deeply creative process.[2] It can alert us to things we should get ready for, remind us of things we had forgotten, but it can also play with ideas for the future and thereby generate entirely new ideas. People that frequently daydream score higher on intellectual and creative ability and have more efficient brain systems.[3] Boredom is a particularly important helper in this regard: as our brain hates boredom, the more bored we are, the more it will entertain itself with alternatives, namely thinking about the future.[4] If boredom makes the brain work out, social media is the sweets that let it sit on the couch.

Not all mind-wandering is pleasant, unfortunately. Sometimes, it can pop up at inconvenient moments—for instance, when you are about to go to sleep, and your mind begins to run through the list of things that need doing. We call it intrusive cognition when we can quite literally not clear our minds from spontaneous futuring despite our best intentions.

Somewhat sadly, companies, societies and governments cannot mind-wander, but different methods can mimic the process. Horizon-scanning and scenario-building are both tools from strategic foresight that allow a group of individuals to look at the future together in an explorative fashion, just like mind-wandering. Explorative means that they do not have a specific task but head out into the future with their minds open to whatever they find.

The first approach, horizon-scanning, is much like when we look out at the ocean and let our eyes wander. As its name indicates, this method tries to increase the range of vision.[5] The movement of the eyes here is therefore similar to the jumps our minds perform when, as individuals, we let them wander. When we scan the horizon as a group, we try to gather all kinds of information that might be relevant for the future we are trying to think about.

Explorative scenario-building is another way groups can mimic the way the mind tells itself stories while it is out on a wander. In scenario-building, like in a bedtime story, the group begins with a starting point and sees where the story goes. Scenarios are like stories for adults: they play with the future to understand possible causal effects, interlinkages and unseen developments in ways horizon-scanning alone cannot. As a policy-tool, they became popular in the 1960s, when the physicist Herman Kahn started using them to think through the potential trajectory and consequences of nuclear war. (He also served as one of the inspirations for Dr Strangelove in the film of the same name).[6]

Although horizon-scanning and scenario-building have become much more popular in policy circles than they used to be, they are still underutilised. That is because most groups prefer the second type of future on-switch: planning, probably because it has a (not necessarily well-deserved) reputation of seriousness and efficiency that looks more fitting for bureaucracies and companies.

Planning the future

Both mind-wandering and planning are future on-switches, but there's a crucial difference: when we

THE FUNCTIONS OF EACH PART

plan, we already know where we want to go or what we want to achieve, and we focus on this and only this. The mind does not jump around by association during planning, but it uses a defined body of knowledge to answer a specific question that is related to a concrete decision or action.[7] Planning is the process that takes us to a goal: by thinking through the different steps that will lead you there, things you need to prepare and perhaps a timeline to calculate how long it will take. Normally, planning makes no room for exploration, imagination or creativity, and it is neither playful nor explorative. In contrast to mind-wandering, it is a process that requires cognitive effort, and it is deliberate rather than spontaneous.

Just think about it: you can easily stomach the idea of hour-long daydreaming but not of hour-long planning! In brain scans, therefore, planning involves far fewer areas of the brain than daydreaming. We find planning easier when we write things down, which has given rise to a whole industry of daily and weekly planners. Planning, and the fashion of using daily or yearly planners, seems like a twenty-first-century phenomenon of hyper-productivity, but it exposes a rather human trait: as early as 500 BC, the Chinese philosopher Confucius noted how important it was for humans to have goals. This may be the reason why the paper planner's history goes back to the beginnings of the printing press. In the mid-nineteenth century, planning one's day in a little notebook was seen as a virtuous act in the United States as it was considered a tool for self-improvement. However, planning was not only about bettering oneself: it was also seen as a tool for happiness. In the 1930s, German economist-psychologist Gustav Grossmann issued the *Glückstagebuch*, the 'Happy Day Planner: An Introduction to Methodical Time Planning' including a 200-page user's guide.[8] Even though it might appear less creative than daydreaming, planning, too, is deeply satisfactory, and studies have shown goal-setting to be hugely motivating.[9]

Which one is better?

While planning might seem a bit dull and boring compared to mind-wandering, the two are complementary. Daydreaming alone will not make that holiday, home ownership or cancer screening a reality—only planning can achieve this. However, planning will not know what goal you should actually aim for—only mind-wandering can formulate that. Companies or governments that plan without mind-wandering miss a crucial opportunity to explore what it is that they actually want to achieve, whether there are other ways to getting there and what else they could do. Collective entities need to have a system in place that can allow for both approaches to futuring, mind-wandering and planning. Conversely, individuals that only daydream without ever planning are unlikely to reach their goal.

THE FUNCTIONS OF EACH PART

One famous example is New Year's resolutions—those that are bolstered by a plan ('work out five times a week') have an almost 50% chance of being implemented, but those that are lofty ('work out more') have an 8% success rate.[10] (The other issue is that we tend to overload the boat: having too many goals at a time means that we probably will not achieve any.[11])

In a way, mind-wandering produces the sketches, but planning brings them to life. Whether you daydream or plan, however, the future mode has now been switched on, and the other parts of the future come into play.

2.2 The present

The present moment appears in the future in the shape of feelings—sensorial experiences and emotions we have about the now.

The second part that matters in the future is the now. This sounds odd as the future is not the present, but it is held together by the present, like two bookends. At the front end, the present gives us information about the future we either want to achieve or avoid, and at the back end, it translates future ideas into actions in the present. This is because the present is the only place where we can have an actual effect on the world around us. This is where we take decisions and implement them, where we throw plates or turn pages, where we engage physically and mechanically with the world around us.

THE FUTURE

Therefore, our future always contains a degree of the present: without it, the future floats around space untethered. A future without a lesson for the present is essentially pointless.

But what is the present? Neurologists and physicists say it is anywhere from 200 milliseconds to 2–3 seconds long, but presentists (those thinking that the past and future do not exist) even say the present moment is eternal. For our purposes, however, it is enough to understand that for most of us, the now is what we can feel with our senses. That is, of course, the obvious five—hearing a song on the radio, smelling burnt toast, tasting ice-cream, holding a warm hand or seeing a rainbow—but that is not all. We also have senses from the inside of our bodies: we feel pain, thirst, hunger, fatigue. In contrast to the past and future, the present is therefore a fundamentally sensorial experience, and the body is the vehicle that anchors us to it. True, we can have bodily reactions to thoughts of the past and future, but they are much weaker than those we have in the present.

Together, the senses do not just give us information on what is going on, they trigger responses in the shape of feelings. It is these feelings from the present that feed into our future: we could feel really unhappy in a certain relationship and thus decide that this will not be the person we want to marry after all, or we could realise that we are not satisfied in our job and use this as the starting point for a career change. We could be envious of our friend's new house and decide to start saving to buy our own in the future or discover that we like photography and decide to take a course in it. We could notice that we miss a friend and arrange to see each other next week. Societies 'feel' somewhat differently, but the mechanism is the same: when people protest against climate change, societies realise something is wrong and changes need to be made; when people vote for a party with a specific take on pensions or healthcare, these are feelings from the present that shape how we see the future. Companies, too, can 'feel' the present: they can look at their sales and ascertain whether their product is a hit, or conduct customer surveys to figure out what consumers want next. All of these are examples of information from the present that serve as signals for what we should do to achieve a certain future.

There's only one hitch: the present can be aligned with what you feel generally about the trajectory of your life, but this is not always the case, and it doesn't come automatically.

The power of too much now

What one feels in the present is not always easy to spot; the now is a rather cluttered space that includes tasks needing to be done, people to listen to, babies to feed, buses to catch and gazillions of Instagram posts to be viewed. Governments jump from crisis to crisis, and companies are busy implementing plans. The hectic nature of the now means that we don't necessarily know whether we still want to go where we are heading. That is a problem because the importance of knowing yourself is not only part of some clever proverb by Sun Tzu but the first step towards generating your future.

Sometimes, we get so absorbed by the present that we even forget about the future. We call this future discounting. This happens especially when we are in crisis as our brain cannot focus on an immediate task and something that is in the distant future; the present takes priority over whatever is next. When we face an emergency—be it avoiding a car while cycling or managing a disaster such as a flood—the parts of our brain we use to think longer term are literally shut off. In this case, the present gives us zero information on the future. It is not only crises that block access to the future, but anything that increases physical sensations—such as alcohol, smoking, drugs, sugar, gambling and sex—does, too. One study showed that students ended up choosing classes depending on how early in the day they were rather than their content, their career trajectory revolving around their need for sleep.[12]

It could be argued that, by doing these things, we take out a loan on our future self who will then have to deal with cancer, obesity, debt and other problems. To be clear, all of us have moments where we discount the future for the present, but some of us have it more than others.[13] Studies have shown that the more we feel 'self-continuity' — in other words, a strong link between who we were in the past, who we are now and who we will be in the future—the closer the future feels, and the less we discount it.[14] This depends, amongst other things, on culture. In one study, the future felt closer to Chinese participants than to Euro-Canadian participants, making it easier for them to bear the future in mind when making choices. It also made them less prone to focalism. Other studies have also shown that East Asians tend to have a lower discounting rate for the future than Americans.[15]

Personal traits such as trust or age also play a role in how much we discount the future for the present. Children under the age of five will find it extremely hard to delay immediate gratification, hence trading the future for the present.[16] However, trust—in the environment, in the future and in the system—is also an important ingredient in counterbalancing the present.[17] Being able to delay gratification is therefore not an inbred personality trait but the result of a world that has taught us to either trust (or not trust) promises and choose the future over the present. Lastly, the capacity to wait is directly proportional to how long we are asked to wait. One study promised adults smaller financial rewards now or bigger ones 15–25 years ahead. Almost all the participants went for the immediate reward, even though the loss was quite substantial.

THE FUTURE

When the future is too far away or we cannot trust it, we will discount it in favour of the present. This applies not just to humans but to societies as a whole: where states can benefit from not fighting climate change today, they will discount the future effects.[18] (When the weather is warm in the present, they suddenly perceive climate change as more urgent than when it is cold—as if they got a preview.)[19]

High inflation will also have an eroding effect on trust, and as a result, economic activity requiring a minimum of trust in the future, such as investments, will go down. At the same time, customers expecting prices to rise will buy more and faster, making inflation even worse. When the future becomes uncertain, visibility shrinks, and we automatically take highly present-oriented decisions.

The other problem with the now is that its information on the future is not always reliable: we tend to overestimate how many features of the present moment will still exist in the future. For instance, hungry people will order larger meals than necessary; planning a holiday during the cold winter might lead to booking an overly warm destination, and people about to take a flight are more likely to sign up for an accidental death insurance if they are scared of flying. Feelings we feel in the present, positive or negative, are projected into the future, but not reliably so. While you are in a relationship, you overestimate how long it will take you

THE FUNCTIONS OF EACH PART

to get over a breakup (because you don't want it), and when you are dreaming of winning the lottery, you imagine it making you happy forever (spoiler: you will not be as happy as you would think).[20] In psychology, we call this the projection bias, which is part of a larger family of biases called affective forecasting bias, a general difficulty with estimating how we will feel about something in the future because we are so tied to the present.[21] There are many reasons for these biases: we underestimate how capable we are of adapting to change (probably because we just don't like it), and we prefer the known to the unknown even if the potential benefits of the unknown outweigh the potential losses—a phenomenon described by prospect theory.[22]

Nevertheless, the good news is that we are not doomed to overdosing on the present. Education, for instance, helps to develop a sense of delayed gratification. In part, this is because the process of studying, while tedious, can earn you good grades later. It is also because education gives you a larger sense of history (why this matters will be explained in the next section).[23] One study showed that smokers invited to think briefly about the future ended up not smoking afterwards: you can therefore actively zero out of the present and into the future. Lastly, the present can be especially useful when used mindfully: 'present-holists'—people that use meditation and present-moment awareness to stay in the now—are in an entirely different category than present hedonists who will discount the future. To them, the present, past and future are all the same, and as a result, none of them is discounted for the other.

2.3 *The past*

The past is a crucial collection of elements we use in the future.

The past is often seen as the opposite to the future, but it is actually pretty much the same thing—at least from a neurological point of view. We now know that the future is put together in the same place in your brain where you keep the past, meaning that remembering the past or imagining the future are two almost identical processes, only in different directions. This also means that the White Queen from the sequel to *Alice in Wonderland* is right when she quips 'It's a poor sort of memory that only works backwards.' Memory is not just for the past—we also 'remember' the future.

Of course, we don't use all our memories to think about the future, but only one specific kind called episodic memory. This type of memory is where we store life lessons as stories, including images, emotions, characters and an overarching narrative—like an episode from a series, hence the name episodic. Remember, for instance, a holiday on the Canary Islands, a painful job interview or the day you got married: they will all appear in your mind's eye like a film. Now imagine that

THE FUNCTIONS OF EACH PART

upcoming trip to Costa Rica or a birthday party—it, too, is like a film in your mind's eye, which is called episodic foresight.[24]

Episodic memory and foresight are directly related: the more episodic memories we have, the more episodic foresight we can generate. That is why young children, teenagers or amnesiac patients will find it hard to imagine a future, precisely because they don't have a database of past memories to operate on.[25] Without a past, no future is possible. Somewhat ironically, this also means that the capacity to imagine the future does not depend on how much time we have left, but how much memory we have gathered: older people are objectively better at imagining the future than children.

Moreover, we don't just use our own experiences for our predictive modelling but also for that of others, people we know directly or indirectly or even fictional characters from films and books we come across. Stories don't merely add data to your database, but they also strengthen your empathy muscle: you can imagine not only your own future but also that of others because of it.[26] (As a plus, stories feel good because your body releases oxytocin while you listen to them, a hormone that helps create social bonds.[27]) Stories of others have a real-life effect on how we model our own future. When Tom Cruise dazzled audiences as a dashing pilot in the 1986 film *Top Gun*, five times more people applied to the US Navy than before its release, and since racing driver Michael Schumacher had a skiing accident in 2013, the use of helmets on slopes has increased from 25% to 83% today. Unfortunately, memories of others have an expiration date: we tend to emotionally absorb mostly those that we heard about during our lifetime. (Which is why almost all knowledge of the 1919 pandemic had expired by the time COVID-19 came around.)

Not only do individuals have episodic memories, but groups or collectives have them too, be it as cities, nations, states or companies: in this case, we call it history. You might not see it as revolutionary, but the development of modern history is perhaps one of the greatest learning accelerators of humanity. Of course, humans always shared stories to learn from each other, and once writing was invented, scribes would write crucial events down. However, it was only in the fourteenth century that Ibn Khaldun suggested that past events could perhaps be interpreted and learnt from. In his 1377 book *The Muqaddimah*, he thereby laid the foundations for modern historiography. This idea gained traction when the printing press was invented a century later, and compulsory education from the nineteenth century onwards meant that everybody who could read could now access the vast knowledge of history. (If this sounds recent to you, it is.) History is, therefore, not merely old stories but a collection of experiences we can learn from for the future.

THE FUNCTIONS OF EACH PART

How to use the past

Then, what do we do with this database of episodes? Essentially, everything we have learnt serves to establish basic 'What If' scenarios: if this happens, then this follows. This makes decision-making a lot faster and easier as we don't have to think through the consequences for every single choice we make. The past serves as a database for the tested and approved, meaning that we tend to repeat the things we like and/or know. That is why we tend to take the same route to work every day, return to known holiday destinations, vote for the same political party as always and buy from the same company.[28] It is also why we might repeatedly fall for a certain type of individual (a process called transference, projecting characteristics from one person to another), or why we want to buy a house that looks like our childhood home.

However, we don't use the past to just repeat past decisions but also avoid them: we vow to never drink tequila again or to go on another Tinder date.[29] Decision-makers do this just as much as we do: every time a political crisis occurs, we turn to the past to find an analogy that could help us. European leaders of the 1930s swore to never fall into the mindset of 1914 again, when they felt that overreaction had led to a catastrophic war—an attitude that led them to the 1938 Munich Agreement (which then was seen as paving the way to World War II). Munich then echoed through the thinking of British leaders when Egypt's President Nasser had seized the Suez canal in 1956, and Suez became an analogy for President Kennedy and his advisors during the 1962 Cuban missile crisis along with Pearl Harbour in 1941 (when Japanese bombers had attacked an American naval base).[30] This list could go on forever: it is universal to imagine different outcomes from erroneous decisions—this is so that we can learn from them.[31]

Whether we establish models, act on stereotypes, develop templates or theories or think in systems, the procedure is always the same: we use information from the past to establish generalities that will apply to the future. This works a lot of the time, but not always, which is why too much of the past can muddle your future. The reasons for this are several.

Too much past

The first reason is that using the past for the future is based on the principle of analogy, essentially the idea that things that look alike are alike. However, as anyone that has accidentally stirred salt in their coffee will tell you, similarities can be deceiving.

In addition, what we consider the past is never complete—in fact, the past as we remember it is just a fraction of what we experienced. Even memories have a shelf life: as a tomato forgotten at the back of the fridge, they decay and rot away when they are not used, even

THE FUNCTIONS OF EACH PART

though at some point they could have been useful. Your database is therefore constantly losing entry points. The same goes for collective history: most things that have happened are simply not known or even will never be known—because nobody wrote them down or passed them on, or because the evidence was destroyed in a war or a natural disaster. This means that we operate on an incomplete sample to establish rules applicable to all.

This brings us to the next problem that we have with the past: not only are we operating from an incomplete sample, but even within the sample we have, we do not use everything equally. Instead, we use mostly what we can remember most easily, a phenomenon called availability bias. You will find it a lot easier to remember political events that occurred during your own lifetime (especially those that took place between ages 20 and 35) and use those more frequently as analogies than others that are perhaps more fitting. For instance, current generations will remember the fall of the Berlin Wall, 9/11 or the Arab Spring with much greater ease than the Suez Crisis or the fall of the German Emperor. It is often said that generals always prepare to fight the last war—rather than to think ahead to what the next one could look like. However, just because we have experienced something personally does not mean that it is the most fitting analogy for the situation at hand.

What makes matters even trickier is that the past is not an eternally frozen collection of facts: it evolves as we go along. This is because our memory is not a videorecorder but a database that we update regularly with new insights that change our predictive models. Sometimes, we make mistakes in the process: for instance, we merge similar memories into one. You might mix two holiday memories together as these trips were very much alike. Other times, our memory changes dramatically: for instance, two studies showed that people recalled the details of how they had learnt of the explosion of the Challenger space shuttle in 1986 or 9/11 completely differently years later.[32] Perhaps to make matters worse, respondents were absolutely certain that they remembered correctly, but certainty is no indication for accuracy when it comes to memory.[33] Your brain is just extremely good at making you believe your own stories.

Unsurprisingly, what happens at the personal level also takes place at the collective level: if you misremembered how you first met your lover, society can equally misremember or misinterpret historical fact. This is not necessarily by evil intention of historical falsification (although that does occur, too); rather, history is not fact but story. How these stories are told depends entirely on context. For example, many ancient graves have now been uncovered to show that women were warriors then too. This has happened in several instances, but the most shocking was the grave of a famous tenth-century Viking warrior whose DNA turned out to show that she had, in fact, been a woman.³⁴ Nevertheless, while historians have come to accept that the analysis and interpretation of what we know of the past is never without bias, the ineradicable idea still seems to be that history is universal and objective.³⁵ There is nothing wrong with rewriting the past: while revisionist history has a bit of a reputation to be one of denial, it is in fact just a normal process of updating a body of knowledge. The point of memory is therefore not accuracy but usefulness for the future. We rewrite our personal or collective past according to what might increase our survival chances in the future.

The past is a useful database, without which we would not be able to imagine the future. When we rely too much on the past, however, we miss out on the fact that the future is not the past and reduce our scope for action. A small current of historians trying to use the past as a large-scale database to spot patterns and predict the future (called 'Cliodynamics'), therefore, should not be taken too seriously.³⁶

2.4 *Thinking the new*

The last part of the future is perhaps the most important one: creativity.

We must use creativity to come up with as many different options for the future as possible, including new ones.

THE FUTURE

Think about it: if you thought about the future without involving creativity, you would think that history always repeats itself. As a result, you would be constantly surprised—not to mention unprepared—when anything new occurred, be it people, companies or states changing their values, minds and behaviours; machines malfunctioning; or extreme weather events occurring. If you relied solely on the past, you would not only be unprepared for unpleasant surprises but also would also miss out on many opportunities. You would turn down Netflix as Blockbuster did (that VHS rental place nobody under 30 remembers) because you could not imagine that people would prefer ordering films from home rather than picking them up from a shop, or you would think that people love film photography too much to switch to digital cameras (so long, Kodak). You would not apply for that job in a different city because you could not imagine a life anywhere else but where you live now; you would not go on dates because you could not imagine that for once you would meet somebody you actually like, and you would not try out new holiday destinations because you could not imagine anything better than what you already know. Your life would be *Groundhog Day* if you relied solely on the most probable.

That is why we need creativity: it goes beyond the probable and explores the possible in the future. Strictly defined as 'the ability to produce or use original and unusual ideas',[37] creativity has three ingredients: it requires imagination (the capacity to create mental images of an alternative present) and originality (something that is new, surprising or different), and it has to be focused on solving a problem, a riddle or offering an idea or vision to a specific audience. Creativity is, therefore, not free-floating but tethered to a concrete question, somewhat in contrast to the image people have of it as an artistic exercise. This also shows on brain scans: particularly creative people have a stronger connection between two areas of the brain that are normally at odds: the area associated with focus and attentional control and that associated with imagination and spontaneity.[38] This also explains why creativity plays a key role in human progress: whenever humans identified a problem and began to think about it creatively, they came up with new and innovative ideas to fix it.

Applied creativity

This started in earnest when humans began to see the future as something that was theirs to shape (see Chapter 1). (Before that, "Innovator!" was actually an accusation just at the level of heresy.)[39] Explorers discovered new continents; scientists innovated in medicine and biology; engineers invented the most extraordinary machines, and authors began to write what is today called science fiction. (The first ones included *New Atlantis* by Francis Bacon in 1617 and *Christianopolis* by Johann Valentin Andreae in 1619). Economists describe the innovative process of business and society in waves, and we are now in the sixth. The first started in the eighteenth century with the invention of waterpower, which then allowed for the invention of machines and the processing of iron, and now we are in the era of digitalisation and robotics. Every innovation created more innovation in its wake. As Isaac Newton put it: 'If I have seen further, it is by standing on the shoulders of Giants.'

That is why science fiction seems to predict the future: all it does is inspire inventors to try what it proposes. On *Star Trek*, a series produced from the 1960s onwards, we can see devices that curiously resemble our mobile phones, tablets or MP3 players. Terms that have only recently arrived in our daily use, such as 'cyber space' or 'Metaverse', first appeared in novels such as *Burning Chrome* (1982) and *Snow Crash* (1992). Virtual reality headsets made a debut in *The Matrix* (1999), and submarines, solar power and space travel all featured in Jules Verne's nineteenth-century novels long before they were actually in use. It's not only science fiction that seems to have an uncanny talent at 'seeing' the future: a set of cards from 1899 imagining the year 2000, drawn by French artist Jean-Marc Coté, appears to show videocalls, 3D-printing and the automation of agriculture and industry.[40] A *Ladies'*

Home Journal article published in 1900 called "What may happen in the next hundred years" predicted digital photography, slowing population growth, ready-made meals and television.

Many of history's most decisive moments have been discoveries of something hitherto unknown (such as antibiotics or an entire continent) or inventions of something previously thought impossible. Exploration and innovation—both of which need creativity to work—are therefore the twin engines that make the future so much more than just a repetition of the past.

How to be creative

In contrast to what some people think, creativity is not something you are born with but more like a muscle that can be trained.

First, thinking creatively relies in large part on what we call divergent thinking. This means thinking about a problem in an explorative and unrestrained way, which is why we particularly like doing it during mind-wandering. During the process, we often use past memories in a new way, meaning that we change the way we look at them or think through what could have gone differently.[41] In contrast to analytical thinking, divergent thinking does not set out to find one solution but several. If you want to try divergent thinking for yourself, sit down with pen and paper and write down all kinds of solutions to a problem; do not stop until you run dry. It is as simple as that, even though it might not come natural at first. When we are creative as a group, we can use tools such as brainstorming or, even better, question-storming: a meeting where people throw in no solutions but questions they have about an issue or a project. Thinking through scenarios, too, is a creative exercise: it invites exploration and establishment of interlinkages, embraces novelty and challenges tacit assumptions. In fact, most foresight methodologies rely on creativity: even trend analysis cannot be done without it.

Quantity produces quality: the more ideas we have, the likelier we are to have a great one amongst them.[42] Just think back to the examples mentioned earlier: amongst the cards drawn in 1899 were some ludicrous ideas such as firemen flying over Paris with batwings or using whales for maritime transport. Most science fiction ideas have not turned into reality, and not every business idea has become a successful venture. Pablo Picasso painted 25,000 pieces of art, but only a handful are known to you, and Walt Disney Imagineering (tasked with inventing new experiences for the parks) have filed more than 300 patents, most of which were never built. Thinking about the future is about creating options: the more we have had, the better we have futured.

Second, creativity is nurtured through diversity of information. This can take many shapes: experiencing unusual and unexpected events makes us more prone to unusual associations or ideas. 'Events' here can be anything ranging from growing up in difficult circumstances or living in a different country.[43] This means that you can actively become more creative by seeking out new experiences, from where you travel to whom you date to what you watch or read. This is, somewhat ironically, especially important if you already know much about a certain topic: the more of an expert you are, the less you can see it in a new way, which is why experts are not better at anticipating the future of their own field than non-experts. In fact, studies have shown that those most capable of anticipating future events were those that 'deploy not one analytical idea but many and seek out information not from one source but many'.[44] This is where the algorithms of YouTube and the like will work against you. By serving you variations of what you already know and are interested in, it puts you on a monodiet of information. If you think of creativity as a sport, you want to cross- rather than over-train.[45]

Third, emotions play a role in creativity, too. People that suppress emotions struggle with imagining the future in general terms. However, somewhat in contrast to the image of the tortured artist, you do not need to be overly happy or sad to be creative; in fact, the contrary is the case.[46] The more intense your feelings are, the less creative you will be. That is because an intense feeling such as disgust, stress or fear will narrow your focus, and as we have seen above, we need a balance between focus and imagination to get creativity roaring.[47] The right dose of feeling to get creativity going is therefore a moderate one, such as mild sadness, amusement, annoyance or boredom.[48]

Last but not least, sleep matters enormously in fostering creativity. It is in your slumber that your brain explicitly seeks out those connections that normally would make no sense, 'like a backward Google search',[49] playing with the available information to see what new it could create from it. Without dreaming, some of humanity's major breakthroughs would never have occurred.

How you feel about the future generally can also influence your creativity. Some of us are by nature more oriented towards uncertainty, meaning that we seek out new ideas and explore unknown possibilities, and others feel more comfortable with the status quo.[50] We also differ on whether we are promotion-focused when it comes to the future, meaning we see it as a place of aspiration and accomplishments, or prevention-focused, meaning we see it as a place from which threats can emerge.[51]

3

HOW TO USE IT

The main problem with the future is that many versions of it exist. The reasons for this are numerous: several future agents—entities that influence the future—in turn have many possibilities all the time, including you and me and your president and everybody else, and even nature and the universe. In other words, the possibilities are exponential, but only one of them will materialise. Simply put: the future is tricky because more things can happen than will happen. Uncertainty, therefore, is nothing but not knowing which of the many possibilities will materialise.

This does not mean we simply have to endure the many things that can happen: we have an operating system in place to (a) make the most of the future and (b) protect us from the worst. In the first instance, we need to figure out what we are sure will happen, a little like a game's rulebook. As a second step, we consider the dangerous side of the future, things that can happen but that would be bad for us, and protect ourselves against it (or not). In a third step, we identify what we would actually like to happen and how to make it come true. Last, we live with surprise: after all, the future will never just be the good or bad we imagined, but it will always include something we did not even think of.

3.1 Almost certainly: What we know

The first thing we do when we operate the future is set aside those things we know or have high certainty about.

Let us begin with some unfashionable news: contrary to what some people say, the future is not entirely unpredictable. In fact, the opposite is true: today, in the twenty-first century, we have more certainty than ever on many things that will happen. These things create the outer rim, the framework within which our future is set. Of course, certainty is not absolute: it is a feeling more than a fact, a high degree of confidence or conviction that something will or will not happen at a certain moment in time. This feeling is based on two elements: frequency—knowing when things happen—and causality—knowing why they happen. Both are elements humans have improved on over time, meaning that today we can be more certain of many things than our ancestors.

When we combine frequency and causality, we get the quadrant of (un)certainty. Everything within the dome is uncertain, but everything outside is rather certain. Our first step in operating the future is to sort everything we know—or think we know—about when and why things happen into this quadrant, separating high from low certainty.

When? Big data, big certainty

For the longest time, we had only one source for certainty: frequency, namely how often and when events occurred. This is what the Sumer and the Babylonians did: anticipating the floods of the Euphrates (remarkably accurate) and divination foreseeing the advent of an event (remarkably inaccurate). All they needed to do was to watch and record their timing and establish patterns on a scale ranging from always to never. Certainty was highest on either end, and uncertainty highest in the middle, like a bell curve. In the absence of understanding the exact cause of a phenomenon, quantity was (and still is) our ally when it comes to frequency: the more often we can observe an event, the more certain we can be about when it will occur.

The first example of this is the discovery—or invention—of life expectancy in 1662. Until then, humans had no idea when death was likely to strike—all they knew was that it would happen eventually. Then, John Graunt, an English salesman of buttons and needles, decided to compile all kinds of details from London's death registry and ran a few averages on it. His book *Natural and Political Observations Made Upon the Bills of Mortality* became a somewhat morbid bestseller because it was the first to make length of life a measurable affair rather than a throw of the dice. His statistics showed that life expectancy changed depending on age: those that had survived the first six years of life had a good chance of reaching 76, and he calculated death probabilities for each age. Based on his idea, life insurances sprang up everywhere, making money on increasing life expectancy from 1840 onwards. Today, death is increasingly reserved for old people, and we are born with a measurable lifespan:[1] as a French woman of 35, you have about a 70% chance of reaching 82, and if you're an African American man, you can expect to live until you're 79.[2] This is a degree of certainty our ancestors did not have.

John Graunt inspired data collection for pattern identification in many other fields, including those that then seemed far-fetched, such as the weather. In the nineteenth century, the weather forecast was so unreliable that it was considered akin to superstition. François Arago, the then-director of the Paris Observatory, even said that 'whatever may be the progress of sciences, never will observers who are trustworthy, and careful of their reputation, venture to foretell the state of the weather.'[3] However, an English officer of the Royal Navy decided to try anyway: Vice Admiral Robert FitzRoy, captain of the ship that carried

Charles Darwin around the world, not only collected weather data wherever he could, but he even invented the term we still use today, 'weather forecasts'. Of course, we needed a lot more data and, later, computers to make sense of them, but the certainty we have today when it comes to the weather is remarkable: the weather forecast is 90% accurate up to five days and 80% accurate a week in advance.[4]

We also use big data in other ways to establish certainties when it comes to an event's timing. While data previously showed no reliable pattern on earthquake occurrence, new data and new computers now seem to suggest that they can be predicted within a three-year window—perhaps still too broad to be an actually useful forecast but a hopeful sign regardless.[5] In other areas, such as predictive policing, big data promises to identify where a crime will occur a week in advance (but not who will perpetrate it).[6] Here, however, as with the search of common patterns when it comes to the outbreak of wars, data will always be limited by the fact that we can never be absolutely certain that we can deduct the future from the past.

What time is it? Creating certainty with common time

We also perfected temporal certainty in another way by developing common time. This means that we all agree on a time and make promises within it for the future.

THE FUTURE

Think about it: without it, we would make appointments with doctors, business partners or friends, but they would not show up. We would buy tickets for airplanes, theatres or football games only to find ourselves all alone at the event. Trains would collide, deliveries of goods would sit idly in ports, grooms would wait at the altar and elections would be held without voters. Without a common system of times and dates, our futures would go off schedule and collide with others; in short, it would be a mess. However, people using common time to announce futures and sticking to it creates certainty. Shops, cinemas, restaurants, doctors, schools, universities, airlines, local transport, food producers and even democracies all announce that something will happen at a certain time, and in most cases, it will. We operate our future on the promises of others to stick to what they announced.

Of course, common time rests on two important ingredients: first, that people actually stick to it, and second, that it actually is the same time. The first aspect depends on culture: being 'late' can mean 20 minutes in the United Kingdom and one hour in Egypt, for instance.[7] The closer we stick to clock time (what is called time discipline), the more we are what is called monochronic. The more flexible we are, the more we are polychronic. It is not clear why cultures differ in this regard, but common explanations are the economic system, religion, nature and social relations.[8] How much you rely on this common time to make your future more predictable becomes particularly apparent when its implicit promise is broken. Think of trains: even though they are remarkably on time (88% of French, 92.5% of British[9]), most of us get upset when they are not. The point here is that a world with common reference points for when certain moments in time will occur makes everybody's future more certain.

The second element is that time actually is synchronised—which it is now, but that was not always the case. Until the late nineteenth century, time was a local phenomenon defined by the sun: when it stood high in the sky, it was noon. In practice, when it was noon in Washington DC, it was 12:12 pm in New York City or 11:48 am in Charleston, South Carolina.[10] This was not an issue because you could not travel to another city so fast as to even notice the 20-minute time difference, and you could not place calls that nobody would take because they were still out for lunch. Thanks to trains and telegrams, however, this changed. Suddenly, both people and information could get to another place fast. Where this became an issue was not so much people having to adjust their watches (if they had any—the watch for all appeared only in the twentieth century), but in the railway system: in the United States, 300 railway operators ran on fifty-seven different time zones, meaning trains waiting at platforms on the same station would have different departure times. One day, an Irish railway engineer named Sandford Fleming missed a train because of this mess and thought up a solution: he proposed to divide the world into twenty-four time zones, each one hour wide or 15 degrees of longitude. It would now be noon in the entire time zone no matter where the sun was exactly. In 1884, the International Meridian Conference held in Washington, D.C. accepted this idea, and today all states have accepted Coordinated Universal Time, which makes it possible for us to coordinate airplanes and Zoom calls across the world.

Common time does not end there: although today most of us now run on the Gregorian calendar (invented in 1582), this has only been the case since the early twentieth century.

The reason it was this calendar and not his predecessor, the Julian calendar, or the Islamic, Hebrew or lunisolar calendar, was primarily its accuracy and therefore predictability: for another 3,323 years, this calendar ties the dates to the seasons without needing adjustment. This was probably its main selling point (rather than its Christian origin). (There's not enough space here to explain the intricacies of time keeping, but just know that the issue with time keeping is that it depends on the sun, moon and stars and shifts around all the time as a result—hence the leap year.) Of course, common time is not foolproof: people do not always stick to it, but the more they do, the more certainty they create.

HOW TO USE IT

Why? The certainty of effects

We have another tool to increase certainty for events that are irregular and difficult to observe in large quantities: causality. This, too, is a rather novel tool in our future toolbox, as we have seen in Chapter 1. Once we understand under what conditions something occurs, we can prepare for an event or maybe even avoid it altogether—a supreme tool in certainty creation.

Our main ally in this regard is science. Since the scientific revolution in the seventeenth century, an avalanche of discoveries has made the world increasingly more predictable. We no longer believe that bad smells cause disease, that pregnancy is the result of proto-humans waiting in a woman's womb for God's word 'go' or that bloodletting will cure a patient of poisonous fluids.[11] There are still plenty of unanswered questions, of course, but many established causalities have made our world—and therefore our future—more predictable.

We also create causality ourselves when we clarify what action will lead to what reaction, commonly called the law. The clearer the law is to all, the more certainty it creates. Of course, humans have had laws in pockets everywhere, but it was their unification and codification that made them certainty-creators, first in Bavaria in 1756, but more famously in France with the Code Napoléon in 1804. The latter influenced many other states in the world to do the same. The law in your country does not simply tell you what your rights are, but it also clarifies what the consequences of certain actions are.

Of course, having the texts is not enough. The more that people trust that the law is actually implemented, the more they feel that they live in a predictable system. That is why the rule of law is often measured not by which texts exist, but by how much people trust those implementing them, such as judges, police officers, defence attorneys and prosecutors.[12]

Together, frequency, common time and clear causalities are your main source for certainty, but they have their limits: uncertainty remains a key feature of human life despite them.

3.2 Live with danger

Danger is managed by maximising our understanding of its nature, its impact and its probability and then taking precautions against it.

In the animated film *The Croods* (2013), a prehistoric family manages the dangers of the unknown by never leaving their cave. The father repeatedly teaches the children that curiosity and innovation are existentially dangerous. 'Never not be afraid,' he repeats. Of course, fear has an important function: it protects us from dangers. Without fear, we probably would not live long: an American woman who was born with damage to the amygdala, the part of the brain that senses danger, lives without fear, and she does not live well: she has been nearly raped, held at gun- and knifepoint and almost killed in a domestic violence incident.[13] Fear looks ahead, sees potential threats and their consequences and makes us take measures to avoid them.[14] It has an evolutionary purpose.

However, not all fears are justified, and not all dangers can be avoided. The only constructive way to live with danger is therefore to actively manage it. We do this by identifying the danger, its extent, possible impact and likelihood, and taking precautions against it. Where we can, we share the burden with others to reduce the possible danger.

Types of dangers

For most of us, danger is an umbrella term for all things that could possibly become a major problem, but in reality, danger exists on a scale: the scale of knowledge. In 2002, US Secretary of Defence Donald Rumsfeld summarised it as follows: 'There are known knowns; there are things we know we know. We also know there are known unknowns; that is to say we know there are some things we do not know. But there are also unknown unknowns—the ones we don't know we don't know'. Although he was much ridiculed for this rather convoluted sentence, Rumsfeld accurately described the danger scale along the most important line: how much we know about it. The less we know about a danger, the less we can manage it. Consequently, we have three different types: uncertainty, threats and risks.

Let us begin with uncertainty on the lowest end of the knowledge scale. Strictly speaking, uncertainty is merely an uncomfortable feeling of not knowing for sure. However, because humans abhor not knowing and crave certainty, they mainly think of it as a space for possible threats. How uncomfortable you feel with uncertainty depends, amongst other things, on your culture.[15]

Threats, in turn, are different from uncertainties in that they are precise, potentially negative, events. In contrast to uncertainty, a threat is therefore something concrete: we can imagine who or what will do something specific that will hurt us. Just like we differ in how at ease we are with uncertainties, we differ on how we perceive threats.[16] Threats are, for instance, terrorist attacks, a disease, an economic downturn or a breakup. There is only one hitch: identifying a threat does not tell us yet what to do about it, how likely it is to occur or what its impact will be. At this stage, we have not managed the danger—we have just imagined it. It is therefore not enough to imagine what could happen but also the extent of the possible loss it would cause.

Threats become actionable when we use them to imagine the risk they pose.

To understand the difference between uncertainties and threats on one hand and risk on the other, it is useful to look at where the term comes from, namely navigation. Its Latin root, risicum and riscus, means cliff or reef. Should a ship hit a reef, it would carry a threat of loss of human life, property and damage to infrastructure or environment. The extent of this depends on the ship's cargo and passengers, as well as the nature of the accident. However, just as a ship is not predetermined to hit a reef, risks are not predetermined to materialise. In other words, risk is calculated by combining the extent of a danger's impact with the probability of it occurring.

$$\text{Risk} = \text{Threat (extent of potential loss)} \times \text{probability of dangerous event}$$

Risk is therefore the part of danger we manage: we measure it, hence the expression 'taking a risk'.[17]

Threat characteristics that increase risk perception

1. Catastrophic potential: fatalities occur in large numbers at a single event
2. Novelty: unfamiliar risks worry us more
3. Lack of understanding: not knowing how an activity or technology works
4. Personal control: if we have no influence over a risk
5. No choice: if we have no say in whether or not we are exposed
6. Kids are involved
7. Future generations
8. Knowing the victim
9. Dread: the more fear, the more risk perception

10. Lack of trust in institutions managing the issue
11. Media attention
12. Accident history
13. Equity: benefits go to some, dangers to others
14. Definite: if damage is not reversable
15. Me: if I am involved
16. Human-made: we are more scared
17. Timing: the closer the scarier[18]

Measuring likelihood

Once we have understood the threat—what it could do to us—we need to figure out how likely it is to happen, which helps us prioritise. Since the Renaissance, when probability was discovered by Italian gamblers, we have used numbers to express how likely something is—or is not—to occur. This is not the place to go into the intricacies of probability theory, but it is enough to know that these numbers are not always as absolute and objective as they look. The probabilities Google shows during a football game are not the same as the probabilities of throwing the number 6 on a die: the latter is what we call objective probability, and the former is subjective. This is also called Bayes' theorem: using numbers to express a belief based on available information.[19] In other words, math is a language, and for most of us, probability is a particularly pesky dialect of it. We might use the same numbers, but we might not mean the same level of risk. When a group of NATO officers was asked to assign numbers to different words commonly used to describe likelihood, they gave wildly different ones. 'Almost certainly' was given a probability of 80% by some and 95% by others. Even so, bear in mind that 75% might mean probable to you but 'very good chance' to somebody else.

Then, with regard to data, risks that we have large numbers of data for can be easily measured, whilst others cannot be quantified as neatly. Some mathematicians think that the absence of quantifiable data equals the absence of sufficient knowledge—in other words, if you cannot measure it, it is not a risk. (Which is why insurance companies often refuse to cover events whose impact or probability they cannot measure, such as space debris or terrorism).

This is a problem as several risks cannot be easily calculated—either because we do not have enough data to say which outcome is the most likely, or what the precise extent of a potential loss is. Just think of the risk of a major democracy collapsing or your marriage: you will have no data points for either—does this mean you cannot think about the probability of this risk? Frank Knight, the economist who came up with the distinction between risks, threats and uncertainties, disagreed: 'If you cannot measure, measure anyhow.'[20] In other words, measurement does not necessarily mean big data and numbers—sometimes, it is just a reflection process on

Share the danger

Once you can calculate a risk, you can do something about it: the obvious first move would be to either remove the danger or take precautions for when it occurs. However, you can do something else: share it. The very idea that risk is something we can distribute amongst people was born in a perhaps unexpected place: Lloyd's Coffee House in London, which opened in 1686. Loitering, coffee-sipping merchants and sailors shared information on water levels, departures and arrivals of ships, and reports of accidents and sinkings; in no time, the owners of the place compiled this into Lloyd's List, which, in turn, others used to come up with a business idea: based on this information, they could evaluate the risk and make an offer on sharing it. Pay me a fee now, and I will pay for the damage if something goes wrong. These risks were initially mostly for shipping, but with time, they extended to others such as burglary, death from gin-drinking or female promiscuity (how this risk was measured, I cannot say). Thus, the concept of insurance was born. (Lloyd's still exists by the way, but as an insurance company rather than a coffee house.)

From insurances for property, it was only a hop to imagine insurances for something even more valuable:

life and health. As data on life expectancy (see previous section) were now available, insurances could calculate estimates on which to base their premiums. In 1752, Benjamin Franklin created the first life insurance company in the United States, the Philadelphia Contributionship. By the nineteenth century, they became common, despite some presbyterian preachers decrying them as 'gambling'. Not long after, universal health insurance was born in Prussia in 1881. Today, 90% of Americans and almost 100% of Europeans have some form of health insurance, and half of Americans have life insurance. (The rest of the world is not so lucky, with half of it having no health insurance).[21] Insurances have some interesting side effects: as they lessen the burden of risk, they create a degree of certainty for the future. This in turn allows for investments, economic growth and stability but also innovation as it makes risk-taking easier.[22]

However, insurances are no panacea for all risks. First, people that are aware of a risk do not necessarily take out insurance against it. In the United States, only about 58% of housing in flooding risk zones are covered by insurance.[23] (More on this in the next chapter in the section on wishful thinking.) Second, insurance companies cannot cover every risk: to them, the risk of life is a business, not altruism; thus, they will not insure risks that cannot be calculated or that are simply too expensive. (That said, for the right price, you can still sign an insurance for a space shuttle or a crashed satellite.) This means two things: insurance cannot cover events that have never happened before or that are so rare that not enough data are available, such as wars, which have been excluded by most non-life insurances since the nineteenth century.

This is a problem because the nature of risk is changing: it has moved from a personal problem to a collective one, and from one we were exposed to into one we create ourselves. While most people died in the nineteenth century from external causes—mainly infectious diseases such as tuberculosis, typhoid or diphtheria—50–70% of Americans now die from ailments in large part caused by lifestyle such as cancer, cardiovascular problems or diabetes.[24] The weather might take us much less by surprise than our ancestors, but our industrial lifestyle means we are now increasing the risks of droughts and wildfires. While we have developed numerous technologies to make our lives easier and safer, some of them have achieved the opposite: with nuclear weapons, humans have invented a tool to eradicate themselves swiftly.[25] To some of us, risk-taking is now even a hobby: since the 1970s, extreme sports such as parachuting or bungee jumping have been all the rage. We have become what German sociologist Ulrich Beck described in the 1980s as a risk society: a society that revolves around the creation and redistribution of risk. Is it a coincidence that the share of insurances in national GDPs has increased so sharply since then?

3.3 Imagine the best

The way to a better future has two steps: imagining things to be different and filling the possibility space with something we want.

Today, we take it as a given that we are entitled to #livingmybestlife, as the Instagram hashtag promises. We sing along to hopeful and positive songs and manifest what we want from life. Indeed, imagining the best is the first step in that direction, but it is neither easy nor automatic for humans. That is because we don't like change: when we have to make a choice between keeping things as they are and changing, we will stay with the same even if the change promises improvement (a phenomenon called status quo bias).[26] As we often lack creativity, we cannot even imagine things to be different from what they are. These two things stand in the way of a better future.

On a large scale, humanity as a whole did not think things could be different or even better until the sixteenth century. Monarchies or variations of them ruled for centuries on end. People did not really change job, social status, or town, and they certainly did not travel to other countries for fun: they were born and died in the same place. Religion looked backwards, not forwards: paradise was in the past, and our job was to return to it; if anything, we would get there after death. Even at the architectural level, more of the same was the norm: most masons involved in the construction of Notre-Dame did not see its completion after 182 years. However, contrary to what some people think, these long-term projects were not the result of our ancestors' supposedly superlong vision for the future: in fact, they had none as they imagined it to be more of the present. The future was a state of more-or-less sameness: it was no currency, no better place than the now. Philosophers of that time shared this idea largely, with Gottfried Leibniz even stating that this was already 'the best of all possible worlds' despite the fact that his contemporary Thomas Hobbes felt that human life was 'solitary, poor, nasty, brutish, and short'.[27] Hume even said that 'mankind are so much the same in all times and places that history informs us of nothing new or strange.'

Then, in 1516, English philosopher, statesman and lawyer Thomas More wrote *Utopia*, a little book describing the perfect life on an imaginary island—if you want the very first work of science fiction, and definitely the first work to think up a world different from the one then in existence. This might sound rather banal to you, but for an official in an absolute monarchy—his boss was Henry VIII, the one with the six wives—this was nothing short of revolutionary. After all, monarchies, more so than other political systems, are built on the idea that they will not change, often because their power was allegedly given by God and is therefore eternal. Thomas More was beheaded a few years later for not attending Henry's wedding to his second wife, but his book remained to set an important precedent: if we can imagine things to be different, we can imagine them to be better—and so, a better future becomes a real possibility, even for us today.

Not more of the same

Then, how do we begin to entertain the idea that things could be different from what they are? As German philosopher Ernst Bloch pointed out in *The Principle of Hope*, this is far from being a given.[28] In part this is because large parts of human life are repetitive and cyclical: most of our daily routine is the same; we live through the same seasons, and every year has 12 months. As we saw earlier, it is also because we like predictability: most people return to the same holiday destination, buy the same products, and order the same dish from the delivery service. Sameness makes life easier as it frees up space for other stuff; thus, in a way, we are wired for it. In another way, however, we are wired for novelty: every time we encounter something new, our brain releases dopamine, which gives us a feeling of pleasure, joy and satisfaction.[29] (Which is perhaps why buying new things can indeed feel good.)

THE FUTURE

Once humans see novelty, they mimic it. If you are stuck in sameness, perhaps all it needs is somebody showing you possibility. Just take the example of Roger Bannister, the first man to run a mile in under four minutes in 1954. Until he broke this record, it was conventionally accepted that it was simply not possible. However, once Bannister had achieved it, people all over suddenly began to run miles in under four minutes: his own record was broken within just 46 days. The same happened to humanity in the fifteenth century, paving the way for Thomas More's book *Utopia*: several events opened the floodgates of possibility. It all started with the discovery of an entire new continent by Christopher Columbus in 1492. Although Columbus was looking for a route to India rather than a continent, he found what was then called the New World. (An odd name if you think about it because the continent was not new on Earth but new to Europeans.) The New World made novelty per se extremely popular.

Columbus' travels had another side effect: contact with other cultures—notably the Incas, who ruled differently (or let us just say better) than European leaders. Conquistador Mancio Sierra de Leguizamo noted, in his testament to King Philip II: 'We found those realms in such good order that there was not a thief or a vicious man, nor an adulteress, nor were there fallen women admitted among them, nor were they an immoral people, being content and honest in their labour.'[30] Shortly thereafter, in 1515, Polish priest Nicolaus Copernicus proposed that Earth was a planet revolving around the Sun like all the others, triggering what is now called the Copernican Revolution: a radically different way of seeing the universe and our place in it. At the same time, Martin Luther challenged the Catholic Church in hitherto unknown ways and triggered, along with John Calvin, the Protestant Reformation.

Of course, more had to happen from there to open the future as 'the time and space of real possibility'[31] as Ernst Bloch put it, but the seeds for understanding that a different world was possible had been planted. Two hundred years had to pass for things to really pick up speed (remember, change was a slow affair then). Enlightenment thinkers began to pave the way with ideas—such as Voltaire, who made fun of Leibniz's and Hume's conviction that nothing could get better than this in his 1759 book *Candide ou l'Optimisme*. Then, the American Revolution and independence gave birth to a new (or rediscovered) political system—democracy—in 1776. Shortly thereafter (if you think 13 years is short), the French Revolution brought the idea to Europe. Both events institutionalised the possibility of change in the most radical fashion: now, even monarchies were not safe from it, removed by human action rather than God. (Now you understand why revolutions scare politicians everywhere: they suggest change is always possible.)

From the eighteenth century onwards, 'not' was increasingly replaced with 'not yet'.[32]

When thinking of a different future, you first have to break with the present, think away from the known or expected and make space for possibility, even the most ludicrous one. This is a conscious effort, not an automatic thing: your status quo bias will tell you that something different is worse than what you have. Knowing that you have this anti-change bias will be the first step; then, seek out information that disproves it, from stories to TED talks to books. Be inspired by change-makers, innovators and people like Bannister that have shaken your world view, and open the door of possibility.

First different, then better

Different does not per se mean better, but it is the first precondition. Once you have opened the possibility space, you can fill it with ideas of how things you would like to see materialise. This part is about desire: what do you, what do we want. This is also what distinguishes utopia from the afterlife: where the afterlife is a given, utopia is filled with what we want. Obviously, what we want changes all the time, which is why utopia is not an end state: it is the actual process of evolving to something better. Once we have reached this better, a new better comes along; as Oscar Wilde put it, 'progress is the realization of Utopias.'

That is why old utopias often contain ideas we find funny—because they have been accomplished already, or because they are not what we want today. Old utopias, such as Italian philosopher Tommaso Campanella's *City of the Sun* (1614), were reflections on what was going on then, focusing on the tension between faith and science, the division of labour, and property. Several books even thought about life on the moon—from English clergyman's John Wilkins' *The Discovery of a World in the Moone* (1638) to Francis Godwin's *The Man in the Moone* (1638) and Cyrano de Bergerac's *The States and Empires of the Moon* (1657)—but they were less about the possibility of space travel and more a trick to talk about better places without offending the governments in place. This changed with the American Revolution: its Declaration of Independence was the first official document to make the pursuit of happiness, a better future, a right in the here and now, rather than a distant place or time. It is no coincidence that the novel *The Year 2440* by Louis-Sébastien Mercier was published around that time, in 1771: it is the first to set utopia within a real country. The protagonist falls asleep in a violent, dirty and poor Paris and wakes up 670 years later only to find a derelict Versailles palace, a parliamentary system, a welfare state and a city filled with enlightened intellectuals.

Although utopias are often sneered at for being unrealistic given that things are extremely bad, they are especially necessary during a crisis; it is not so much a happy state that gives birth to it, but an unhappy one.[33] If today, on average, humans live longer, healthier and freer lives, it is because people before them imagined how things could be different.[34] Remember how we said that the present always features in how we think about the future? It is from here that we know what we do not like, and conversely, what we would like. Knowing what we like is easier said than done; that is why states and companies conduct surveys, and for us as individuals, pain or dissatisfaction, but also envy or admiration, can be a guiding star. Sometimes we need some inspiration, which is where science fiction is useful: seeing sliding doors, iPads or flying taxis inspires us by showing us that things we desire are achievable. These are the two elements we need to fill the future with some highlights: first, we need to know what we desire, and second, we need to see them as achievable.

In 1922, French psychologist Émile Coué developed a method to trick the mind into seeing things as achievable that are not in immediate reach: his book *La Maîtrise de soi-même par l'autosuggestion consciente* posited the idea of the self-fulfilling prophecy, by which repeatedly telling ourselves that something will happen will bring this about. This is also how positive thinking, the law of attraction, visualisations and even the placebo effect in medicine work. Athletes using mental imagery—essentially visualising the act of performing their sport—improved significantly; for instance, jumpers performed better 45% of the time, and shooters 23%.[35]

This is because when you imagine a positive future for yourself, your brain will pin it to its board of expectations[36] and then align your behaviour with that expectation. Every time something happens that goes against that expectation, it is recorded as an error in the frontal cortex. Instead of concluding that the objective cannot be met, the brain concludes that not meeting it is the mistake, and adjusts behaviour accordingly. This also explains why optimists live 15% longer than pessimists regardless of other factors, including socioeconomic status, body mass index, social integration and alcohol use.[37] As optimists expect the future to be a good place, they automatically make choices that make it a good place: they smoke less, exercise more and pursue goals that they enjoy into very old age. Optimism also helps us delay gratification: our future self is worth making a sacrifice for in the present.

3.4 *Live with surprise*

We have three ways to deal with surprise: prevention, reduction and adaptation.

Even with the best of preparation and imagination, the future will always contain elements that we did not see coming—either because we did not expect them at all, or because we did not expect them to happen in that way. Be it the Arab Spring, the financial crisis, a health diagnosis, an accident or a call from an ex, surprise is part of life, and learning to deal with it is a major element in managing the future; but what is it?

First, surprises are not negative per se, even though we often talk about them that way. They can be good (winning the lottery), neutral (discovering that Swaziland is now called Eswatini) or bad (being attacked by Russia). For our brain, it makes no difference, it always has the same response to something unexpected: freeze. In normal circumstances, this should take about $1/25^{th}$ of a second, but it may vary. The reason for this freeze is that our brain pauses as it realises that something new and important is happening.[38] In a second step, it launches into 'find' mode in search of an explanation for what just happened. In a third step, it updates or shifts our world view (or finds an excuse not to). Last, we talk about it: sharing a surprise with others is one of its key features, and the more they are surprised by it, the more they will share it, too. This part plays out both in person—telling my friends how somebody returned my lost credit card—and in the news, which is dominated by surprises and attempts at explaining them. In fact, the very word 'news' hints at this need to share novel experience with others. Perhaps this is also because surprise is always an intense emotional experience: positive surprises produce great joy, and negative ones terrible anguish. Some say that an element of surprise increases any type of emotion by 400%.[39] (Although I doubt this applies to the Swaziland/Eswatini surprise). The bigger the surprise, the stronger the emotion[40]—which is why we like to max out the good surprises by hiding behind sofas at surprise parties, but prepare people for bad ones by saying things such as 'I have something difficult to tell you.'

No matter whether positive, neutral or negative, dealing with surprise is a tiring task for the brain, like a complicated mathematical riddle, and the greater the difference between expectation and surprise, the longer this process takes and the longer it will take to respond to it.[41] This applies as much to babies learning to use a new toy as it does to policymakers. How fast governments introduced measures against COVID-19 depended largely on how surprised they were by it. States that had already experienced something similar were less surprised and consequently on average 19 days faster at introducing measures against it.[42] The temporary freeze surprise induces can even be used as a strategic advantage: whether Japan's attack on Pearl Harbour or the Egyptian-Syrian attack on Israel in 1973, they used the short-term advantage of surprise as it paralyses the other side for a short while during which the battlefield will be essentially deserted. (Ultimately, surprise attacks do not have a convincing success rate, however—not because they do not work, but because they are generally chosen by the weaker party.[43])

As surprises can be positive or negative, we both like and dislike them. We like them because our brain releases dopamine when good ones happen, giving us feelings of pleasure and satisfaction. This is also why we prefer sports games with high uncertainty to those with lower ones (such as football).[44] However, we also dislike how surprise exposes our vulnerabilities. (A feeling the Holiday Inn tried to capitalise on with the slogan 'The best surprise is no surprise.') A large-scale negative surprise can produce substantial shock as we must review our vision of the world in an existential manner.

Whether we like or dislike surprises in general has to do with our personality types. People that are extroverted, adventurous and spontaneous tend to like them, whereas those who are introverted and anxious tend to dislike them. In either case, however, both the positive and negative effects of surprises are always temporary: lottery winners are not substantially happier than they used to be once they got over the first rush of dopamine.[45] The best way to handle this aspect of the future is to learn to live and cope with it.

Surprise prevention and its shortcomings

Surprise prevention is the method of dealing with surprise that most of us are already familiar with: we take out insurances, build intelligence services, avoid new people and events and always order the same dish from our favourite restaurant.

Sure enough, surprise prevention has its place, but it also has its drawbacks. First, too much surprise prevention is not good for you either: it is not just boredom but a form of stress—what scientists call hypostress, which correlates with depression, drug abuse, gambling, aggression, relationship dissatisfaction and academic failure. (Or simply put, what we all felt during the COVID-19 lockdowns.) Second, surprises—serendipitous surprises—open doors to all kinds of things, from meeting a handsome lover to breakthroughs in science (Teflon, antibiotics and Viagra were all discovered by chance).[46] However, perhaps most importantly, surprise prevention alone does not work: it can never prevent all surprises, and it does not make us better at dealing with them when they do appear. Accepting that surprise is part of the future is perhaps the first step in being ready for it: the least we expect surprises, the longer it will take to adjust to them.

What we can improve on in this regard is two things: reducing the impact of surprise and adapting once it is there. Surprise reduction does not mean preventing surprise altogether but lessening its impact by mentally engaging with a potentially surprising event before it happens. This is easier than you would think as only a small fraction of events are actually what futurists call

Black Swans (an entirely unpredictable event), such as that regretful ex calling, a random accident or a rare disease.[47]

For many other events, somebody, somewhere, always saw things (or variations of them) coming and making use of them is the best way to reduce surprise. The point here is less getting the potential event exactly right—although that would be great—but rather to mentally walk through the corridor of possibility at least once. Just thinking about a potential surprise will reduce its magnitude, and with that, our response time. One way of doing this is scenario exercises (essentially thinking through 'what if' situations), which have been shown to reduce bias in thinking about an event and its outcome and increase decision quality.[48] Another is subscribing to a prediction market and regularly making predictions of future events, later reviewing how well one did. The more we practice thinking about the future and reviewing our past assumptions, the more we expose our biases and improve our capacity to deal with surprises once they are there. (Examples of such markets are Good Judgment Inc., Metaculus and Hypermind.)

Bias is what stands mainly in the way of reducing surprise: to get to the information that could give us a warning, we need to learn to listen better. This is not just the case for us but also for decision makers: in most cases, long response time to a new development—be it a pandemic, a cancer diagnosis or an invasion—is not the result of no warning but of a lack of belief in the warnings.[49] That is why the 'who saw it coming and why did they not prevent it?' debate is entirely futile.[50] No intelligence service, strategic foresight report or early warning system can be stronger than human biases that hold a worldview together. When American President George Bush claimed that the CIA had not warned him of the collapse of the Soviet Union, when France's president Emmanuel Macron claims climate change was not predictable or when the then EU's top diplomat Josep Borrell swears that the world is made up of unpredictable events, they are simply wrong.[51] Just like the rest of us, they have a brain that chooses to filter inconvenient things out—and unfortunately, the older we get, the better the brain gets at doing this. That is the problem with surprise: it has more to do with you and your biases and filters, and less with the level of available knowledge.

Lastly, the best way to handle surprise is to adapt to it. After having lowered the initial freeze time with surprise reduction, we need to respond in a new way called improvisation. When we mobilise unused resources or use them in a new way, we create and act at the same time. First, we should accept that the surprise is there—denial will only make us lose time. Second, we should be creative with the tools and means we have as they may be used in a different way. Third, we should not get scared, or we will freeze—we ought to embrace the process. Finally, we should stay optimistic: some of the best developments do come out of surprises, even negative ones.

4

SAFETY INSTRUCTIONS
WHAT NOT TO DO

We can mishandle the future in several ways, but the reason for this is always the same: every time we are particularly uncomfortable with the fact that the future is uncertain, we resort to one of four faulty mechanisms to make the discomfort go away. These are: catastrophising; its twin, wishful thinking; creating an illusion of certainty; and imagining outright fake futures.

The problem with these mechanisms is not just that they are wrong but that they make us vulnerable to dangers: we misread causalities, therefore getting unexpected results; we think we know what is happening and therefore do not pay attention to other possibilities, good or bad; or we get so scared—or are convinced that the best will happen—that we do nothing. Whenever you notice yourself making use of one of these future substitutes, be therefore extra careful: your future is now more at risk than ever.

4.1 Catastrophising

Catastrophising distorts our perception of dangers and paralyses us.

As we have seen earlier, humans have a fabulous alarm-system that is designed to protect them from dangers lurking in the future: fear. However, this alarm-system has a major problem: when it goes into overdrive, it malfunctions. Too much fear is no longer fear but catastrophising—overestimating the probability of a negative event and exaggerating its negative consequences. It can manifest itself as anxiety, phobia or even panic attacks and paranoia. In contrast to fear, which is a rational, cognitive process, catastrophising is a biased, emotional one—and as important as emotions are when it comes to the future, too much of them can have a range of negative effects (see also the next chapter on wishful thinking).[1] This is also how catastrophising is different from worst-case scenario thinking even though the two sound similar: the latter is thinking through a scenario with undesirable features as one of several possibilities and should result in concrete steps to be taken against it. It is therefore a useful and important tool in future-proofing ourselves. However, catastrophising does not have much to do with rational thinking, and even less with taking action.

The issues with catastrophising are several. The first one is that it will not necessarily protect you: no direct link exists between how much we fear an event and it actually occurring.[2] In fact, we often just fear things we hear a lot about or that are especially emotionally charged, rather than those that are particularly likely. One example is the fear of dying in a terrorist attack: during the heyday of Islamic State terror, we were scared to take the metro or go to a Christmas market, but the odds of dying in an attack are minuscule: 1 in 964,531 in the United Kingdom and 1 in 1.6 million in the United States between 2001 and 2017.[3] Instead, your odds of dying are much more likely to be from a heart disease or cancer (1 in 5),[4] but I am sure you have never been as scared of a heart attack as you have been of the Islamic State. In the same category are fearing Earth being hit by an asteroid (1 in 74,817,414) or satellite debris (1 in 21 trillion), both of which regularly make headlines even though they are highly unlikely to occur.[5] More often than not, we tend to catastrophise in crime, too. Women tend to worry much more about being assaulted on the street than young men, who are twice as likely to be assaulted.[6] (Women are much more likely to be assaulted at home: 1 in 7 women and 1 in 25 men have been hurt by their partner.) It is also common to mutter that crime has gotten worse, although crime statistics show that it has dramatically decreased in the last half-century.[7]

Catastrophising says a lot about how vulnerable we feel, but it is no indicator for reality.

The inaccuracy of catastrophising

For one, we overestimate the probability of rare events in general.[8] Media exposure plays a major role in our over- and underestimating of events we should be afraid of. That is because the world we see in the media overemphasises negative events: 10–30% of its content is violent crime, and 31% is war.[9] However, other content, such as natural disasters, will also traumatise us by proxy just by watching the news covering them.[10] (Mass media and social media show no difference—both amplify negative events significantly.)

How likely we are to overestimate negative events also depends on our personality: the more sensitive we are, the more neurotic and pessimistic and the more we are likely to overdose on fear. Of course, elements such as where we live, how old we are, what cultural background we have and what gender we identify as also play a role: people aged 18–44 are twice as likely to be anxious than people over 60, and women are nearly twice as anxious than men.[11] (A separate category is post-traumatic stress disorder, where people that have experienced a traumatic event are stuck in the emotional processing and relive it repeatedly. In contrast to other catastrophising, the cause for this is a real event in the past, not an imagined event in the future—somewhat ironically, tending towards catastrophising before the event makes it more likely to experience this disorder.)

Why catastrophising is bad for you

Not only is catastrophising not particularly accurate at predicting future dangers, but it also has other negative effects. For one, it does not feel nice physically: it makes us sweat; causes our hearts to race, and our stomachs to ache. It is also bad for our physical health, making us more prone to heart diseases, sexual dysfunction, insomnia and ulcers.[12] People with chronic pain who catastrophise will experience even more severe pain.[13] Mental health suffers too: in addition to post-traumatic stress disorder, catastrophising makes us more vulnerable to obsessive-compulsive disorder, eating disorders and some psychoses.[14] Catastrophising in love means we attach anxiously to our romantic partner, as 20% of us do, making us more prone to stress and, ironically, more likely to pick a partner that will not give us the security we want (another 23% avoid love altogether from catastrophising intimacy).[15]

Perhaps most importantly, catastrophising slams the breaks on all things future. The reason for this is that during catastrophising the amygdala can 'hijack' our brain by blocking access to those areas that are responsible for problem-solving, imagination, motivation, learning and memory. In this mode, the brain pulls all tricks to immobilise us: we move into avoidance, lose motivation and freeze. When we overdose on fear we will not be able to think clearly, come up with a creative solution, be able to access important memories ('where is the fire extinguisher?') or maintain objectivity and perspective.[16] (This is why emergency plans should be practiced until they become routine, meaning they are no longer stored in a part of the brain that the amygdala can block access to.) As a consequence, we take the hands of the wheel that the future is: we stop imagining and choosing it. That is why the cost of seeing danger in the wrong places is mostly the cost of inaction: we do not go on dates; we do not apply for jobs for fear of failure; we do not go to the job interview, or when we do, we sabotage ourselves. We do not invest money in promising funds for fear of losing it; we do not visit exotic and interesting countries for fear of flying or the unknown culture, and we vote for anybody promising the same as yesterday. Catastrophising is to the future what botox is to your forehead: paralysing poison.

Catastrophising has another cost: overlooking the real dangers because we are so focused on our imagined fears. A lost American boy scout hid for four days in the woods from the rescue workers looking for him because he was following his parents' advice to not talk to strangers.[17] After the 9/11 attacks, many Americans avoided flying, taking the car instead. However, driving is inherently more likely to lead to accidents than flying, and it is estimated that 2,300 people died in car accidents because they feared taking the plane.[18] A similar process is at play when it comes to gun ownership: in the United States, many people buy guns because they are afraid of other people with guns, but statistically, the evidence shows that the real risk is not other people with guns but your own, with which you might hurt yourself intentionally or by accident.[19]

The list goes on: once the fear machine is in motion, it is difficult to suspend it to think about the best options.

Of course, some people take advantage of our tendency to catastrophise: politicians. They can take our fears of strangers, criminals and loss of identity and spin them up into full-blown catastrophic thinking. US President Trump and his play on fears of immigration and crime are one example, but he is far from being the only one. Right-wing parties seize the fact that most Europeans vastly overestimate the share of Muslims in their populations as a result of xenophobia.[20] US Senator McCarthy's hunt for (pretty much imagined) communists was not called the Red Scare for nothing: it played with a common fear people had and whipped it out of proportion. Our tendency to catastrophise can be even used as a weapon against us; the repeated references to Russia's nuclear weapons by President Putin are not to be understood as actual messages of intention: the catastrophic fears these words trigger are themselves the weapon.[21]

Whenever somebody triggers your worst fears, be aware that catastrophising might be here. Take a step back—if you cannot, turn to Chapter 5.3 for more instructions.

4.2 *Wishful thinking*

When we succumb to wishful thinking, we replace rational analysis with a good feeling that is not actually good for us.

Too much negativity is not good for the future—but too much positivity is not either. It is one thing to hope—having an idea of something we want or do not want to happen—but another to fall into wishful thinking. How are they different? Take this (very common) example. Suppose we buy a lottery ticket for €2. We hope to win the jackpot because we could finally go on that trip to Japan we have been dreaming about (this is called desire). We are perhaps even optimistic that we will win: after all, only those who play can win, and we may have heard of this one woman who even won the lottery twice. In none of these feelings—hope, desire or optimism—is absolutism; they carry doubt, possibility but also uncertainty.

Wishful thinking has none of this ambiguity, and it is absolute and certain: we will win the lottery—ignoring the fact that the evidence for thinking this is pretty thin: our chances are 1 in 292.2 million, less than being killed by lightning.[22] When we give in to wishful thinking, we use desire to replace facts. To make it worse: the more we want something, the more we overestimate the likelihood of it happening.

All of us are guilty of wishful thinking: it is a deeply human trait regardless of age, gender or culture. It can apply to both positive and negative things, meaning we can be sure something positive is certain to happen and turn a blind eye to things that are inconvenient.

In the brain, wishful thinking can occur in three different ways: by not paying attention to things that contradict it (such as the lottery odds), by interpreting things in a way that suit us (we lost this time but we will win next time) and by responding to things as if wishful thinking was true (we will play again). The problem is that this process can unfold over and over again, regardless of how many times we have done this before, as wishful thinking is rather immune to the learning effect we get with other mistakes due to its emotional charge.

Hope dies last

The list of examples where wishful thinking takes over our rational mind is endless. One example is love:

precisely because we are infatuated, we overestimate the odds of a relationship. Wishful thinking also plays a role in sex: men generally overestimate the sexual interest of women, and women underestimate the sexual interest of men.[23] Wishful thinking makes us convinced that we are right, whether in a court room or a bedroom, creating more conflict in the process.[24] Confusing hope and fact also appears in sports: football fans continuously expect—and even bet—on the victory of their teams and are notoriously wrong regardless of their level of expertise.[25] The more attached fans are to their teams, the more convinced they are of its victory regardless of past performance.

It is the same in politics. Voters are normally convinced that their favourite candidate will win in upcoming elections, overestimating the chances of their favourite party or candidate by 4 to 1, and the more attached and invested they are, the more they will overestimate. (Especially if they are poorly informed, they will rely mainly on their feelings to shape their expectations.)[26] In 1932, 93% of Roosevelt supporters predicted Roosevelt would win, and 73% of Hoover supporters predicted Hoover would win.[27] (Roosevelt ended up winning with 57% of the popular vote.) As George Orwell once noted, 'people can foresee the future only when it coincides with their own wishes.'[28]

Wishful thinking also regularly makes an appearance in the world of finance, where it is often called the 'this-time-is-different syndrome'. People can fall for the same patterns of wishful thinking over and over again, meaning they will overestimate the value of assets or chances of an innovation. Both the 1990s dotcom bubble and the 2008 American housing bubble are examples of this.[29] Although much has been made of the greed that drove these bubbles, wishful thinking is an even stronger mechanism, blinding successful investors ranging from Elon Musk to Thor Bjorgolfsson (whose Icelandic bank Landsbanki went bust when the bubble burst).[30] Regular people are not exempt from this: homeowners generally overestimate the value of their properties by up to 20%.[31]

The price of irrational hope

Why do humans have this positive bias? The simple answer is because it feels good. We apply wishful thinking for outcomes we desire; thus, imagining they are certain or already here makes us feel good. The problem is that this happens particularly when things are not only uncertain but critical. We need money from the house sale to finance an operation; we would probably die if disaster struck, and we are really in love with that person—all are situations where we really need the result to be the way we want it to be. The more emotional we feel, the more we can be tempted to indulge in wishful thinking. Of course, it might be useful in some ways: surfing on its confidence, we can be tempted to make a move on the person we like, convince people of a project or take a leap of faith.

However, wishful thinking comes with a price tag.

First, it means that we stop questioning the situation, looking for evidence and testing assumptions. We are stuck in our wish, overestimating certainty of success and rewards, leaving us vulnerable to all the scenarios in which our desired outcome does not materialise. We think we will be better and need less time or resources for a task than actually will be the case.[32] The so-called planning fallacy is why 90% of manuscripts are handed in after the deadline (not this one though!), why almost all of us are late with tax declarations and why building projects (from Berlin's airport to Sydney's Opera House) are completed years later and at a much higher cost than anticipated, while in IT, just a third of projects are delivered on time.[33]

Second, wishful thinking also means that we underestimate risks even though we are fully made aware of them—this is what futurists call a Grey Rhino, an event of which warnings were ignored (and a cousin of the Black Swan we met earlier).[34] Most people that live in a zone prone to disaster do not have adequate insurance against it. The 5 million people who live in the zone of highest volcanic risk in the world in Southern Italy where three active volcanoes are located not only have no insurance but also no adequate evacuation plans.[35] Similar thinking played a role in underestimating the size of a possible tsunami that could hit the Fukushima Daiichi Nuclear Power Station (which then materialised in 2011). The list does not end here: regular people underestimate their personal risk of heart disease even though it is the number one cause of death.[36] The war in Ukraine was given a 40% chance of happening just a month before the invasion—despite there being intelligence warnings of more than 100,000 Russian troops amassing at the border.[37] When one of Bernie Madoff's investors was warned that these investments were fraud, he replied, 'If you are right, then I am a dead man'—and gave in to wishful thinking instead. (He lost $1.4 billion in 2008 and committed suicide in his office.) The most tragic example of wishful thinking is, of course, climate change.[38] Wishful thinking is not the only reason why humans decided to ignore the consequences of their industrial activities, but it was the emotional fuel in the tank of all those denying it even existed. It simply was easier to think the evidence was wrong.

Lastly, when we realise our wishful thinking does not reflect reality, we must deal with the outcome: if we were expecting our football team or our party to win, we may get angrier or sadder than is warranted. If we denied a risk and it materialises, we are in for a shock, and it takes us much longer to respond and adapt than had we thought about other scenarios. When we are behind on deadlines, we become frustrated and stressed.

4.3 *The illusion of certainty*

Certainty is an optical illusion: it looks like a fact but is a feeling.

We like making fun of people that fell flat on their face with their certainties, whether it is IBM president Thomas Watson dismissing the potential of the computer ('I think there is a world market for maybe five computers') back in 1943 or Microsoft CEO Steve Ballmer's dismissal of the iPhone ('There's no chance that the iPhone is going to get any significant market share. No chance.')[39] However, neither you nor I are safe from the dangerous mechanism that was behind these mistakes: certainty in our beliefs and opinions that give us the illusion that we already know how this ends.

The problem is obvious: we do not know how this ends. We can guess, have an inkling, or have reason to think something is likely, but we cannot be certain. Certainty might feel like fact, but it is a feeling—a nice one because it gives hope and security, but still, a feeling that has no evidence, no proof, no fact. That is because it is not the result of a reasoned conclusion but of active filtering of information that contradicts it. The more emotional you feel about something, the more you do it. Paradoxically, this means that the more certain you feel, the more likely you are wrong. (Yes, read that again.) Certainty is not optimistic or pessimistic per se, its defining feature is that it has no doubt about where it goes. Of course, a little dose of certainty here and there does not do harm—I might feel certain that I will find a parking lot next to the restaurant or that a political party will do well in power—but when we overdose on certainty, we become fatalistic, lazy, blind to alternatives, intolerant or even violent and vulnerable to dangers, surprises and changes. Nothing makes us as vulnerable to surprise as certainty: the bigger the certainty, the bigger the surprise.

Second, the much bigger problem with certainty is that it stifles thinking about other options. Being certain that democracy will march on might make you lazy when it comes to protecting it, believing that war is no longer a possibility will make you vulnerable to those wishing to hurt you, and believing that progress has only one face means you do not see it when it materialises in other forms.[40] Any time you encounter certainty when it comes to the future, your alarm should go off.

Then why do we keep falling for it? There are two reasons for this. The first is—as with the other faulty mechanisms in this chapter—that certainty, even an illusory one, takes away the uncomfortable feeling of uncertainty. The second is that certainty can make an uncomfortable present more bearable if it is declared to be part of a larger existential story. By linking something out of our influence in the present into the long future, we can at least tell ourselves that we are part of a larger meaningful story. In addition, this kind of long future extends our natural, 100-year-long perception of the future beyond that date and makes us aware that we will be responsible for what it will look like. Being certain that this future is not far but in fact imminent might feel loony to some, but what it really does is indicate a sense of urgency when it comes to actions in the present—although admittedly, it could also serve as an excuse for doing nothing.

The definite end of the future

Certainty about the future comes in various forms, but all of them have ideological zeal in common. (We have seen this before: the more emotion, the more wrong we tend to be when it comes to the future.)

One concept which lends itself to it is the end times or the apocalypse (strictly meaning 'revelation' in Greek), according to which humanity will go through a series of catastrophes and crises and then the world as we know it will end. As a basic idea, it exists in pretty much all major religions, whether in Buddhism, Judaism, Christianity, Islam or the Old Norse religion (only Taoism has no end time concept). In all of them, the end is preceded by a series of signs—often scary and weird, such as dragons or horsemen—which will announce the great reckoning when God will judge humans by their deeds. However, while the end times sounds like the end, it actually is a new beginning: afterwards, either hell or paradise awaits, or the whole thing starts again. It is therefore not to be confused with scientific deliberations on when the sun will stop burning (in 5 billion years), the effects of climate change or even potential effects of a nuclear war: the end times is a spiritual moment of reckoning, a punishment from God for bad human behaviour.

The end times as such, a distant and unknown point in the future, is not where certainty is problematic: as we do not know when it will happen—in fact, all major religions have banned speculation about the precise moment—it is not infused with absolute certainty. However, delusional certainty appears when people are convinced that they know when the apocalypse will happen. This type of certainty has a long history: the earliest recording we have of a group believing the end was imminent was in 66 AD, and countless recordings have been made since. Even today, conviction that we are living in the end times is more frequent than you might think: 39% of Americans—including nearly half of Christians (47%)—believe this, and 83% of Afghanis, 72% of Iraqis and 68% in Turkey expect the end times to begin within their lifetime;[41] 41% of Americans are convinced that Jesus Christ will reappear before the year 2050;[42] and 20% of British people said the government should have contingency plans for a religious apocalypse.[43]

In 2012, when the end of the Mayan calendar led to another end times heyday, 14% of the people in the world were convinced that they would witness the Armageddon.[44] (Armageddon sounds scary, but it just means 'battle on a hill outside Jerusalem'.) Europe seems to be the exception: one German poll resulted in 46% saying 'nonsense' and 31% saying 'possibly'. Only 10.5% were sure of it.[45]

While it might be easy to make fun of people who are convinced that the end is indeed nigh, the concept is regularly used and abused by radical groups. Nothing creates cohesion as much as the conviction that a group is chosen by God, who is the only one that knows what lies ahead. The Islamic State is only the latest to build its entire existence on the idea that not only are the end times coming, but that it is itself one of the signs preceding it. Before you get scared: such groups appear regularly in history when times are particularly hard and distressing. In the 1960s and 1970s, when fears of a nuclear war were running high, groups such as Peoples Temple, the Manson Family, the Branch Davidians and Heaven's Gate all claimed to know when the end was coming and what had to be done. Japanese cult Aum Shinrikyo gained strength during the country's economic crisis in the 1990s. All these groups ended up killing either themselves, and/or their opponents, en masse.[46]

The most important thing to understand about apocalyptic movements, big or small, is that they do not know more than you do about the future. All they know is how to give the current crisis much greater meaning by inserting it into an existential story about humanity, thereby making it more bearable.[47] This is why we have moments in history where millenarism is popular and others where it is less so: when things seem bad or overwhelming, some of us will resort to fake knowledge to make it easier to cope.[48] Needless to say, the fear of the end times is also a profitable enterprise: televangelists in the United States are selling survival kits with the slogan 'Imagine—the world is dying and you're having a breakfast for kings,' and insurances are offering coverage against zombies or major upheaval.[49] Whenever you feel tempted to buy into this, stop, review the facts and carry on.

The definite direction of the future

Radical groups pretending to know the end are not alone in their certainty: anyone pretending to know that things will get better might be different in tone, but their facts are just as sketchy. In contrast to the apocalypse, this is a more recent concept and was born alongside the discipline of history. As mentioned in Chapter 1, history was just a list of facts, until the idea of metahistory was born in the seventeenth century. This is essentially the conviction that human development does not just bob along randomly but has a direction towards something better, what is commonly called the philosophy of progress or *Fortschrittsglaube*.

The first to do this was the Italian philosopher Giambattista Vico in the seventeenth century: he thought that nations underwent phases in history, but he was not clear on whether this was cyclical or spiral, or whether an improvement occurs over time or not. Others got on board with this idea; French revolutionary Marquis de Condorcet predicted in his *Sketch for a Historical Picture of the Progress of the Human Mind* unlimited progress in science, technology, morality and society, including equality of races and sexes, and peace between nations. Most famously, German philosopher Georg Wilhelm Friedrich Hegel developed a whole philosophy in which he posited that history was not merely a set of successive events but a process that would lead to the freedom of humanity. 'The question at issue is therefore the ultimate end of mankind, the end which the spirit sets itself in the world.'[50] Do note that Hegel did not say that this journey would be a smooth one or a linear one.

Up until Hegel, philosophers had explained how things were in the now, without giving much attention to the future. One person in particular was not happy about this: Karl Marx. In 1845, he wrote, 'The philosophers have only interpreted the world, in various ways. The point, however, is to change it.' In this spirit, he also wrote that 'the victory of the proletariat [is] inevitable' as the capitalist system would ultimately implode.[51] (Hence the Soviet joke 'The future is certain; it's the past which is unpredictable.')

We can give Marx credit for describing the patterns of production and wealth and outlining some developments that indeed did materialise, such as the mechanisation of work or the spread of capitalism across the world. However, the certainty with which he predicted an end to all classes and even states in themselves caused tensions in more ways than one. States that were not Marxist were scared by it; states that followed it used different degrees of intolerance and violence to implement it. In communist states such as the Soviet Union or China, thinking about the future was mostly limited to planning: since the future was already known, deviating from it by imagining alternatives was almost considered heretical, especially during Stalinist times. Miloš Zeman, who later became President of the Czech Republic, even lost his job in 1989 when he published an article presenting the future as a plural space of possibility; in Romania, a brief opening under Ceaușescu was quickly stifled when the dictator realised the future was a dangerous box full of ideas he could not control.[52]

A variation on the theme of certainty is Francis Fukuyama, who wrote *The End of History and the Last Man* in 1992 (note the reference to Hegel's end of humankind), which posited that the great struggle between political systems was over and that, as Hegel had predicted, democracy would be the model all societies would aspire to as the freest. Fukuyama, Marx and Hegel all have received a lot of criticism and ridicule for predicting a future that did not entirely materialise—but this is not the main issue with their ideas. There are two reasons why their ideas are problematic. First, if we use history as the source for analysis, how wide do we set the angle? When does history begin, and where are we looking? Most metahistory has used the last 5,000 years of human development as a frame, and most of it has looked primarily at the Western world. More recently, Big History looks at humankind as a whole within the universe and uses a much broader lens. Yuval Noah Harari's book *Sapiens: A Brief History of Humankind* is one example of trying to understand human history more generally, but it is not the only one. Even so, history is interpretation, not a source of certainty.

The good news is that you can dismantle certainty by questioning yourself, by seeking out information that contradicts it and by spelling out your assumptions and defining under what conditions you would change your mind. Those of us particularly capable of this have been shown to excel in forecast tournaments where one has to make predictions about future events—all it takes is a bit of agility of the mind and some letting go of ego.[53] You can spot certainty overdosing when terms such as 'always', 'never', 'everybody' or 'nobody' appear, and when no conditional verb is in sight. Somewhat paradoxically, certainty overdosing occurs precisely in those areas where uncertainty is strongest, where we have little solid data and evidence, such as the spiritual and the political realm, perhaps precisely because the stakes are high.

Of course, certainty appears regularly in the medical field; so far, however, no innovation has been able to predict exactly what your future will hold when it comes to health—or even personality, for that matter. While the discovery of genetics originally led to the hope that one day we would be able to decode exactly what our personal future in terms of health would look like, so far, this has not materialised.[54] Futures here can only be given in probabilities, not certainties.

4.4 *Fake futures*

A whole market of fake futures will sell you anything to make you feel better about the future.

Just like fake Gucci handbags and knock-off watches exist, so do fake futures: future tools that look like the real thing but are in fact bogus. As these tools are not the result of science, studied causality or reasoned reflection, the chances of them not actually helping you to make better decisions relating to the future (which is what any future tool should do) are especially high.

We have two types of fake futures. The first one sees the future as the result of forces outside of our control. This thinking dates back to the Babylonian idea that the future is a written, fixed thing that we cannot influence but that we can foretell to some extent by looking at unrelated events and tools that precede it. This type of fake future is the dominant one—perhaps because until the seventeenth century, it was the norm to think of the future as something we could not influence rather than the other way around, which is a more recent development.

The other type of fake future is where we think we can influence the future by taking steps that are not related to it. This is what we call superstition—nothing but the conviction that a causal link exists between two events that in fact is not there: examples are thinking that walking under a ladder, seeing a black cat crossing the street, spilling salt or saying 'Macbeth' in front of actors will all bring bad luck. The numbers 13, 14 and 17 are considered bad luck in so many different cultures that most airlines have removed rows with these numbers. Similarly, carrying an amulet or talisman or eating lentil soup before midnight on 31 December are all said to bring good luck in different cultures. These examples are all European and American, but numerous variations exist elsewhere: in China, the number 8 is considered lucky, whereas having a moustache is unlucky.[55] In Egypt, walking under a ladder is said to give you strength, leaving footwear upside down will bring you misfortune, and in Russia, putting empty bottles, keys or change on the table will lead to financial loss and tears. The list goes on.

However, none of these fake futures, regardless of their form, have evidence (as in complying with the scientific method) for them actually seeing the future or seeing a way to influence the future.

Horoscopes

Just take horoscopes, perhaps the most famous kind of fake future, which we discussed in Chapter 1. Invented by the Babylonians in 500 BC in what is today Iraq, their basic idea is that the star constellation at the time of our birth will determine our personality and life trajectory, and to make things easier, they broke these constellations down into 12, which are now called the zodiacs. (Actually, there are 13, but the Babylonians felt that 12 sounded neater. If you are born between November 29 and December 17, you would—in theory—not be a Scorpio or a Sagittarius but Ophiuchus.[56]) From Babylon, the idea travelled all over the world; thus, you will find it (or variations of it) in places such as China and India. The hitch is that, even though horoscopes are wildly popular, no proof exists that they work whatsoever.[57] In studies, astrologers were not capable of matching horoscopes to individual personality profiles, and 95% of people found a random horoscope that they were told was theirs to be accurate—when in reality, it was the horoscope of French serial killer Marcel Petiot.

Horoscopes are not the only type of fake future. Premonitions or premonitory dreams have no higher accuracy rate either: during a 1966 experiment in the UK, *The London Standard* (formerly *The Evening Standard*) ran an experiment called "The Premonitions Bureau." It collected more than 700 precognitions, of which just 3% (18 in total) later came true. Neither tarot cards (which appeared in the fourteenth century in Italy but started being used for fortune-telling only in the eighteenth) nor psychics, crystal-ball reading (first century BC in Ancient Rome), palm-reading (300 BC in what is today India) or tasseomancy—reading fortunes in tea leaves or grounded coffee—have any way of proving that they have a reliable way of devising the future either.

Yet these fake futures are fairly popular: in the United States, 37% of women and 20% of men believe in astrology, regardless of whether they believe in God or not, as do 43% of women in Germany;[58] 69% of American women and 39% of American men admit to having contacted a psychic,[59] and 18% of American women and 8% of American men admit to feeling uneasy with a hotel room on the 13th floor.[60] In the United States, searches for 'tarot cards' and 'how to read tarot cards' went up 31.9% and 78.4% during the pandemic.[61] How much a society is prone to fake futures depends on how much it has adopted science as its standard for establishing causalities—where this is not the case, superstition fills the role of science.[62] This also explains why astrology was one of the seven arts all students in Europe had to study—until the seventeenth century, when it was superseded by science.

Falling for fake

Then, how come our otherwise fairly decent foresight system falls for a set of tools that do not have any evidence of working?

There are three broad reasons for this: first, we not only desperately want to understand causalities, but we hate nothing more than when we do not understand why something is occurring. Randomness is to the brain what garlic is to vampires: it makes it recoil in horror. Therefore, our brain will look for confirmation, for patterns, and it will find it in the oddest places. Finding one makes us feel good (a bit like a fake Gucci handbag can) as it makes an uncertain world more certain. This is what happened to the 95% of people who recognised themselves in a murderer's horoscope. This phenomenon, called the Barnum Effect, occurs when we recognise ourselves in particularly vague statements (such as 'at times you feel very sure of yourself, while at other times you are not as confident'). It works especially well when the statements are positive ('people admire you'), when we think they apply only to us (which is the case for horoscopes as they are based on our birthday) and when the person making them is considered an authority (such as a famous astrologer).[63]

The second reason why we may fall for fake futures is related to the first: when we find a pattern that can help us make sense of the past, present and future, we feel like we are in control. This is why people that feel powerless, or that have limited power, tend to resort more to fake futures in order to deal with the feeling that they have no or little influence over their future. This is one possible explanation for why women, who generally feel less powerful and influential than men, are more likely to read horoscopes and consult psychics. Regardless of gender, people that are in greater need for approval such as those who are anxious, self-conscious and depressed tend to resort more to fake futures. This could also explain why American millennials and Generation Zers—two generations struggling with existential angst and powerlessness—are the most disposed to rely on these tools—33% versus 21% of Americans over 65.

The third reason why we may resort to fake futures is because they make us happy, which makes sense given that they provide a feeling of certainty and control. One study showed that reading positive horoscopes increased positive interpretation of events, cognitive performance and creativity, but only in people that felt they had no sense of control beforehand.[64] Fake futures can also give us hope: in 1854, when spiritualism was all the rage, the utopian socialist Robert Owen emerged after a sitting convinced he had spoken to the spirits of Benjamin Franklin and Thomas Jefferson. He was sure they had told him about a glorious future for humanity (which he later wrote down in *The Future of the Human Race; or Great Glorious and Future Revolution to Be Effected through the Agency of Departed Spirits of Good and Superior Men and Women*). Owen was sure that spiritualism was going 'to prepare the world for universal peace, and to infuse into all the spirit of charity, forbearance and love'.[65]

Then, what is the problem with fake futures, you ask? Just like with wine, moderation is key. Reading a horoscope here and there, not sitting in row 13 or not wanting to 'jinx' a desired outcome by talking about it are harmless little acts to manage the feelings of uncertainty and lack of control we have when it comes to the future.[66]

However, just like red wine, too much of fake futures is dangerous. When we use these tools instead of taking our future into our own hands, we outsource responsibility, opportunity—and we will have to deal with losses. In Japan and Korea, a zodiac particularly bad for girls led to an increase in abortions in 1966.[67] In India, couples will marry according to their astrological match, even though evidence shows no link between divorce rates and astrological 'compatibility'.[68]

Some are intent to take advantage of our need for certainty, even when it is fake. In New York, an astrology centre charges up to $1,000 per consultation, thanks largely to its claim that it can predict stock market plunges, and a financial software charts celestial movements and correlates them with economic data.[69] Given that 40% of Generation Z think astrology can help them make better financial decisions, this is a lucrative market—despite the lack of evidence. Fertility psychics are a whole new market that has emerged recently, making money from women desperate trying to conceive. A much older but similar concept is the medieval Catholic practice of selling indulgences (essentially guaranteeing a place in heaven), revived by several televangelists in the United States who promise success in business, love and health in exchange for a donation. If you need another reason to lower the dose on fake futures: relying on them seems to correlate with unflattering personality characteristics such as narcissism, authoritarian tendencies and low levels of intelligence.[70]

5

TROUBLESHOOTING

The future can work like a well-oiled machine, but even in the best cases, it can be in need of repair. This is nothing to be worried about; in fact, every future needs to be revised and updated occasionally, even in the absence of crisis or fear. However, even though it is normal, it is never comfortable: as the future is so important for our happiness, our direction and meaning in life, tending to it for revision, relaunch or repair, is always fraught with discomfort.

There are four ways in which the future can be in need of troubleshooting: the first is when it has come to a natural expiration (i.e. is no longer needed or valid). The second is when we cannot even see it, meaning we are in a state of depression. The third is when we can see it but see only scary and sad things. Lastly, the future can be in need of repair when we have no idea what we should actually fill it with.

THE FUTURE

5.1 *When the future has expired*

We constantly generate new futures, but occasionally, the system stops because they have reached a natural endpoint.

Futures are living creatures, and as such, they can die; or perhaps, instead of dead, we should say they have expired: they are no longer useful, feasible or desirable. This is perfectly normal but sometimes not easy to live with.

Futures reach their natural endpoint in various ways. The first is when they are behind us in time. In this case, you will most likely barely notice that they have disappeared. The longing for a holiday; the dread of an exam; the anxiety before a flight; the excitement at the idea of one day buying a house, falling in love, getting married or having a child—all forgotten and gone up in smoke once they are done and dusted. For individuals, it is no different than for societies: we forget that we used to be worried and scared of the hole in the ozone layer, terrorist attacks or recessions or that we were excited at the prospect of shorter work weeks or a currency we would be able to use in many different countries. The reason for this is that futures have a distinct purpose, namely, to inspire decision and action with regards to a concrete event or development. Once this purpose has evaporated, it makes most sense to cast them aside, to basically declutter your brain. You might still be able to recall past futures but only with some effort: many people do not even remember what they wanted to do professionally as kids. (The exception to this is existential fear: if you were in absolute terror about the idea of your plane crashing, that feeling will be easy to recall.)

Some futures reach an endpoint differently: when our values change, how you feel about the future will change, too. You will remember from Chapter 1 that the present is part of the future: who we are in the now will influence what we want next. As we and our context change, it only makes sense that our futures change along with us. When I recall the goals I used to put on my bucket list as a teenager (parachuting, working in a Kibbutz, shaving my head, just to name a few), I find none of them desirable today. I do not need to prove my courage—in fact, I am scared of jumping out of a plane; I prefer surfing over working on a socialist farm, and shaving my head turned out to be a rather unflattering idea. However, more generally, this also applies to bigger futures, such as getting married, having children or working a certain job. We might have wanted them or rejected them at some point and then change our mind about them as our values change.

What applies to us as people also applies to companies or societies. When you look at old, futuristic ideals, you will discover that people found things that we now find abhorrent desirable, or conversely, that they considered things that we covet undesirable. One article from 1900 was jubilant at the idea that in 2000 we would all eat ready-made meals—which many of us are, but nobody considers this progress.[1] Living in a high rise, as often seen in science-fiction films, was once considered the epitome of the future (and still is for some, if you look at Saudi Arabia's urban mega project The Line), but for most people today, access to nature and beauty is especially important to their wellbeing.[2] (In fact, the whole notion of wellness only appeared in the 1960s, well after the beginnings of futurism, and therefore does not prominently feature in early ideas of what an ideal world would look like.) We now want mosquitoes and flies to be around (predicted to be exterminated in the article from 1900), lament the loss of community and find driving a car to be reactionary rather than a symbol of progress as it once was.

Letting a future die

Regardless of what the values that have changed are, letting go of the old future can be disorientating at first. The reason for this is that your values—and by extension, your future—give your life direction and order. Like a handrail on a staircase, they guide us and give us stability in the turmoil of life. When they change, this creates instability by definition, but when they change for something unfamiliar (or worse, something we used to dislike), it gets complicated. The thing is, however, that nothing about this process is wrong or unnatural: it is normal. One study showed that every seven years or so, humans undergo what we call a 'crisis' but is, in actual fact, just a process of reviewing one's values and synchronising them with one's outer life—in other words, we update our future.[3] (Which is why crisis indeed just means decision in ancient Greek: it means deciding on which direction to go in.) Perhaps the most famous one is the midlife crisis, but it is a bit of a misnomer: crises can (and will) occur several times throughout life, not just in the middle. This process is so normal that never having a crisis simply means being particularly talented at pretending not to have one. It is also important to note that not living in line with one's values and following the expectations of others was the number one regret of people on their deathbed, according to a palliative nurse.[4] Delaying a crisis just means it will be even more momentous when it finally breaks out.

At society levels, we also face crises when we let go of an old future. Just as parts of us are still attached to an old future, parts of society might still be attached to one. (Which is actually where the terms 'conservative' and 'progressive' originally come from: preserving what is versus moving towards something new.) You can spot the death of a societal future by the intensity of the emotion that permeates the debate around it, often going near ideas of identity and history and playing with fears and hopes. Often, those still attached to the past will refer to it ('Make America great again'), and those done with it will refer to a new beginning.

Futures can expire in a third (and potentially rather painful) way: when they are simply no longer possible. In contrast to the previous case, this death is not our choice—it is because the main ingredients of a future are no longer available to us. It could be things like being rejected from a job, being dumped by our partner or losing our money. It could also be more existential: people we love passing away or falling ill, or our own health failing us. Whenever we lose a key ingredient to our future, we do not just lose this—an entire future goes with it: the images of a certain career, of being together on a beach in Costa Rica or in front of an altar, or of a house in the country all wither away in front of our eyes. Futures where we see ourselves being superb skiers or footballers disappear as we learn that our knees will never recover, or, in an even more dramatic case, a more severe health diagnosis will call all futures into question.

At society level, futures can be taken away, too. Our economy might collapse; our environment might change, or, worst of all, a natural disaster or a war will wipe out all kinds of futures we had imagined for us as a society. War is therefore not merely traumatising due to death and destruction but also because it causes futures en masse to die.

TROUBLESHOOTING

How to re-initiate the future

Whether the future has to change due to an internal adjustment or an external one, it is a discombobulating process, but do not despair: humans are extraordinarily good at adjusting to change and creating new futures. Just look at these numbers: 61% of men and 51% of women experience at least one traumatic event in their lives (such as a disaster, an accident or assault), but only 8% of them will experience post-traumatic stress syndrome, and of these, about half will recover within six months with therapy.[5] However, even more will actually undergo post-traumatic growth, experiencing higher happiness levels than people that did not undergo this crisis. The point here is not to belittle these severe experiences but to show that with the right care, many—if not most—of us can adjust to changes and even come out better for it. Losing the ability to walk, for instance, takes a severe psychological toll, but 58% of patients said they were happy most of the time more than 10 years later.[6]

Here are a few things you can do to let go of the old futures.

The first is to acknowledge that change is here and that you do not like it. Resisting and denying change is the first reaction for most of us when futures are slipping away from us: we cling to hope that our ex will come back, that this affair will peter out, that a miracle cure is available for our illness, that the company will not let us go or that climate change might be a hoax. However, the longer you keep denying, the longer the process will last, and you will get stuck in the birth canal of a new future.

The second is to grieve the end of this future. For many people, pen and paper works best, but any outlet to express all the reasons why you liked this future and what you will miss about it will do. It could be the image of you being a youthful rebel, companionship or a feeling of financial comfort. (Do not go for the actual ingredient you have lost, like your wife or your money, but the feeling that the ingredient gave you. This matters as, while the ingredient is gone, you can still look to recreate the feeling somewhere else or in a different way.) Whatever it is, write it down and give yourself a moment to be sad about it being gone.

The third is the acceptance of the old future being gone. Whether Buddhist or Stoic wisdom helps you, surrendering to the things in life we cannot change is part of the process. As philosopher Marcus Aurelius said, 'Loss is nothing else but change, and change is Nature's delight'. Change is not good or bad in this logic, it just is.

The fourth is not to jump straight into creating a new future—acknowledge, grieve and accept first. A new future will begin to generate itself automatically once this process is over, but artificially launching one just to skip the pain will make it inauthentic and therefore not sustainable.

Lastly, as always in crisis, maintain life hygiene: eat well, work out, see your friends and keep your hands off drugs or heavy drinking. You need to be as stable as possible to navigate this change. Of course, if this change is a gargantuan task, do seek professional help: there is no need to suffer alone when psychologists and life coaches are there to accompany you through it.

5.2 *When we cannot see the future*

Sometimes the machine simply cannot come up with a future.

You might think the worst thing that can happen to a future is for it to be a negative one, but in reality, the punk movement of the 1970s summarised it best: having no future is even worse than having a bad one. When we cannot even generate a bad future, a part of being human is broken. It means we stop thriving, moving, evolving, deciding, doing. We stand still in the present—not in a good, mindful way but in a sad, paralysed one. There are many reasons why we can lose our inability to conjure the future, but rest assured: this can be remedied.

At the personal level, having no future expresses itself as sickness. Remember how we learnt in Chapter 1 that thinking about the future makes us happy? It is only logical that not being able to do so makes us sad. Depression is in fact nothing else but the inability to imagine your future, the conviction that one is not an agent of change and that one's goals are unattainable.[7] Although sometimes portrayed this way, depression is not a character trait that some people have and others do not; instead, it is a common phenomenon that impacts one in three women and one in five men at some point in their lives. Women are likelier than men to experience it, and older people more likely than those younger, but this differs by country. In the United States, for instance, 17% of people between 17 and 29 said in 2021 that they had experienced major depression in the last year, as opposed to 5.4% over the age of 50.[8] How long depression lasts varies significantly—on average, about six months.[9] Depression is not a 'civilisational' problem: in the absence of sufficient data on depression, one may have the wrong impression that poorer countries are happier. As you read this, 5% of people—about 280 million people around the world—are going through a depressive episode. Where depression is not treated, it can lead to suicide. For 700,000 people each year, depression, the lack of a future, makes life so meaningless that they take their own lives. Suicide is in the top 20 causes of death worldwide.[10]

Living without the future

Many of us experienced a lack of future during the pandemic. The lockdowns in particular suspended the future, especially in the early days: every day was the same; we had time horizons of weeks and months only, awaiting governmental announcements, and we had an unclear existential threat in the virus. As a result, depression rates went up by 25%.[11] The lack of future the pandemic induced for all of us is similar to what's felt by some when they are stuck in a situation from which they cannot escape. In Sweden, children of asylum-seekers that had to wait months, sometimes years, to get an official decision on their status developed what was called 'resignation syndrome': they stopped eating, drinking, talking and walking. Having no future effectively meant having no life.[12] That is also why inmates have generally high depression rates: their lack of freedom, lack of agency and repetitive days mean that their future is not even imaginable. In American prisons, almost a third of inmates had signs of depression.[13] While statistics on depression in European prisons are not available (let alone standard agreements on how to treat it), the existing numbers on suicide rates in German, French and Austrian prisons are much higher than anywhere else.[14] The most extreme case in this regard is death row syndrome: inmates that know that they will be executed but do not know when, often spending years—or even decades—in a suspended, future-less state. To take back their agency and escape their lack of future, many commit suicide.[15]

If you get the feeling that depression is becoming more common, you are not entirely wrong: an increasing number of people are going through depressive episodes—but because the world population is increasing and more people are talking about it. On average, the percentage of people with depression has remained the same since the 1950s—refuting the idea that wealth could fix all mental ailments.[16] We do not have statistics on how frequent depression was in the old days, but we do know that it was a known phenomenon. The ancient Greeks prescribed hot baths for it, and during the eighteenth and nineteenth centuries, it was known as melancholy.

Restart the future

Then, what does this mean? Perhaps temporarily losing the ability to imagine one's future is as human as having one in the first place. This is important because a stigma still exists when it comes to depression, as if it were abnormal or even the result of having a weak personality (as 30.7% of Americans said in a survey).[17] This explains, in part, why most patients go through depression untreated: half of people in Western countries and even three quarters of people in the rest of the world.[18] That is an absurd number for a disease that is treatable, and the earlier the better before it becomes chronic.

Both the treatments for and the forms of depression vary, and not one treatment works for everybody. In large part, this is because we have not fully understood where it comes from, but progress is being made all the time.[19] Medication works for many people, as do lifestyle changes. Therapy, too, has proven to work, and it has come a long way since the nineteenth century, when it was first developed.

Whereas it was (and still is in many places) standard to talk about one's past as the source of one's pain, future-oriented therapy focuses precisely on the fact that depression comes with the inability to imagine the future. Instead of talking about our parents' divorce, it wants you to develop stories about who you will be, on positive goals, to get the future engine in your mind working again.[20] Just thinking such thoughts might get the hormones that make you happy flowing again.[21] Whatever type of therapy you choose, however, the important thing is that you act on depression and do not let it linger.

Collective depression

It's not only individuals that lose the inability to imagine the future; societies and groups do, too. We do not call it depression but other things: age of uncertainty, polycrisis or permacrisis (the word of the year in 2022). No matter what we call it, the symptom is the same: we no longer manage to generate a future, and it does not feel good as it paralyses us.

There are two broad conditions under which this occurs: the first is crises that require our immediate attention. Remember our discussion in Chapter 1 about how we can never be in more than one time at a time?

THE FUTURE

Anytime something requires our attention in the here and now, we leave the future. If too many things happen in the here and now successively, it is almost as if we get homesick for the future because we are forced to stay in the present. It also means that we do not do anything about future crises: not because we do not care but because we simply cannot. (Somewhat absurdly, staying in crises excessively therefore generates even more crises.)

The second condition under which this can occur is when the range of possible futures is too large, and we do not have the necessary knowledge to grasp them. This can happen when there are many actors and causalities in a specific future and when these are not well understood. Whenever people talk about complexity, this is what they mean: a system that they have not understood (yet) because it is not clear who does what and with what effects. If you feel that we live exactly in a time like that, then you are right: we have lived through several successive crises whose exact effects we could not foresee, and we had to stumble forward with our decision-making because we did not really know what to do.

The good news is this is not the first time we find ourselves in such a situation. In fact, just like many of us will suffer from a depression at some point in their lives, it is not unnatural for a society or company to lose its ability to generate a future. The last time this happened in Western societies was in the 1970s. Books with titles such as *Future Shock* (1970) and *Age of Uncertainty* (1977) were bestsellers. Crises such as the Yom Kippur War and the oil shocks (1973 and 1978), the Watergate scandal leading to the resignation of President Nixon (1974), the attacks on Israeli athletes at the Munich Olympics (1972), the rise of left-wing terrorism all over Europe, the toppling of the Shah and the Iran hostage crisis, where 52 Americans were held captive in Tehran for over a year (1979), are only a few examples. Like today, inflation rates were soaring—14% in 1979 in the United States—and an energy crisis was unfolding. Before the 1970s were the 1930s, and before that were other crises.

None of this means that we should not take this situation seriously; however, we should remember that we are wrong to think this is a unique moment in history, and to tell ourselves that we cannot cope, as we can. Every time a system becomes more complex and difficult to understand, we need to learn and adapt and lean into the uncertainty to determine what the possibilities are. However, to do that, we need to switch our future engine back on just as we have before. Human beings hate uncertainty and change, but they are very good at both. In fact, we need surprise, spontaneity and change to grow and become better.[22]

We can do that in several ways. As governments, we develop tools to think long-term, for instance by developing anticipatory governance structures. This is a fancy way of saying that instead of running from day job to day job, institutions regularly use strategic foresight. This is a tool whereby multiple futures are developed to see which ones are possible, desirable or avoidable and then used to make decisions. (A little like future-oriented therapy, but for states.) You would perhaps say, shouldn't government always do that? Yes, but in reality, this practice is not as well established as it should be.[23] Most governments operate on one future and plan for it. That is one of the reasons why they keep being surprised when things turn out differently. The states where anticipatory governance has been developed to some extent are Finland, France, Portugal, Spain, the United Kingdom and the United States—but more can be done in all of them. Of course, getting a society out of its 'No Future' attitude is not just the job of governments but also societies. Getting together in NGOs, schools, universities and companies as artists, writers and citizens to talk about the different futures and how we can get there also helps restart the future engine. We need to learn to redefine uncertainty not as a loss but as a possibility space over which we have influence. Once we understand that we have choices, we lift the veil on the future.

5.3 *When the future is bad*

Sometimes, even with optimism and hope, the future is simply bleak.

TROUBLESHOOTING

We all know what a future gone bad looks like: it is one that elicits difficult emotions from us, such as fear or even anger. In some cases, this can break the very concept of the future. Why? Too much fear does not actually propel us into action but freezes us; thus, instead of shaping the future with the decisions we make today, we end up doing nothing. On a small scale, we call this procrastination: delaying actions or decisions. Or when we do act, we can actually make the negative future happen—a phenomenon called self-fulfilling prophecy.[24] A classic example of this is driving away a lover with one's jealousy, caused by fear of losing them. In medicine, this is the nocebo effect: patients expecting a medication not to work, or for pain to increase, have a good chance of experiencing exactly what they thought they would.[25]

Of course, not every negative future will be equally dramatic. Dreading the upcoming lunch at your nosy in-laws will most likely have no negative repercussions on your quality of life, for the simple reason that (a) it is a future with a short lifespan; (b) it will most likely be nicer than you thought; and (c) you have the freedom to not go (at perhaps the price of a fight with your partner).

How bad a particular future feels depends on three elements: when the future has a particularly long lifespan, when its impact on us is overwhelmingly negative and when we have little influence over it. However, there are steps to remedy a bad future, and I don't mean denial (this is a popular option, but I don't recommend it).

The first thing to do is to tone down the intensity of your negative feelings about it. This depends on how bad you are feeling. In some instances, you might just feel dread, but in the worst case, when you experience true terror of a certain future, your brain is being hijacked by the amygdala—a part of the brain that is responsible for triggering fight or flight (we saw this earlier in Chapter 3). This comes in handy in some situations, but not here, where neither fighting nor fleeing will solve the problem. The problem is that it blocks access to all those parts of your brain that will help you: those responsible for reasoning, logic and creativity. The way we get our brain back to 'normal' is by doing anything that gives it a sense of security: walks in the forest, petting an animal, working out, cognitive behavioural therapy or taking a bath. Believe it or not, science has found that watching superhero films increases wellbeing, too.[26] It really does not matter what it is you choose—the important thing is to switch the glaring alarm off, or otherwise, you cannot think.

Then we use our mind to reframe our thinking about this future. By changing how we think about a certain future we can change how we feel, and we can find ways we can influence the future and move back into action.

TROUBLESHOOTING

How to handle a bad future

Take a pen and paper and follow these steps. First, write down everything you think you know for sure about the future in question. Second, write down how these thoughts make you feel. Set the feeling list aside—we do not need it now. Third, ask yourself what information this thinking is based on. Fourth, go out and find sources that make your picture more detailed, but be careful: avoid information that will terrorise you even further. One way to do this is to look for answers that are specifically about you: where you live or who you are, for instance. This way, your brain, which is an information-addict, will get the feeling that it understands it better which should immediately make you feel better. Look at everything you have collected and write down all the assumptions that you have about this information. For instance, you could assume that they will never change, that they are indisputable or that they are even false. No matter what they are, write them down. This way you will realise that your thinking is based on assumptions which may or may not be true. In the next step, find solutions that others have come up with for your problem. Now, review what you have and look at the blanks: what are we missing? Write down the things that are still unknown about the future. This is the possibility space, and seeing it immediately should make you feel better, too. Now, reformulate what you think about the future: 'this will not happen if...'. Then, find action space:

what actions can you take to make another future possible? Last: get going! The more passive you are about a future, the worse you will feel.

Now let us use these steps on a few fears that are fairly common today. A highly popular one is climate change, which ticks all the boxes of a critically negative future: its effects on us will be mostly negative (unless your ambition is to grow wine in Normandy); as individuals or individual states, we have little influence over it, and the entire planet is affected. It is also a bad future with a pretty long lifespan: all the way to 2100 it is projected to get worse; thus, it is not only bad for us but also our descendants. A highly common thought that people have about climate change is that it will lead to the extinction of humanity: 37% of Germans, 45% of French, 33% of British, 21% of Danish, 24% of Swedes, 26% of Finns, 28% of Norwegians, 43% of Spaniards, 41% of Italians and 38% of Americans think that the extinction of humanity as a result of climate change is quite or very likely. Numbers are even higher in Asia: 55% of Chinese, 71% of Indians, 65% of Thai and 67% of Vietnamese think we are essentially doomed.[27] People in Asia and the Pacific are likelier than Westerners to think that it will lead to a new world war.

As a result of this thought, many of us have pretty catastrophic feelings: all over the world, 59% of young people are very or extremely worried, and 84% are at least moderately worried. More than 50% reported feeling sad, anxious, angry, powerless, helpless and guilty.[28] Now let us go to step 3: review what the sources say about the extinction of humanity as a result of climate change. Is there actually evidence of a global war or humanity going extinct? Where have I heard this? You will probably find that some scientists indeed call for more work on the possibility, but no evidence shows that humanity as a whole will go extinct as a result of climate change.[29] There's also no evidence to show that a war will break out: science still does not know when wars actually start. Do more research: ask yourself, what is the worst that can happen to me and to my town or region? Make it as concrete as possible for you. Now run an assumptions check. What do I assume about this information—that it is absolutely correct and no new information can change it? Under what conditions would I have to change my mind? For instance, we could say we will change our mind when new science comes in that says we have more certainty about climate change or conflict. Now, go and research the proposed solutions. Here, too, make it as concrete as possible: look at concrete projects, even in your area. In your next step, write down everything we do not know for sure yet about how climate change will pan out: will there be tipping points or not? Will humans find new ways to reduce CO_2 emissions? Now look back at your initial thought (e.g. 'humanity will die because of climate change') and reformulate: 'humanity will not die as a result of climate change if...'. Lastly, find action space and get going. Does this mean we can sit back and relax? No, but it shows we have an influence on this, and that is what we need to tackle the problem. Your fear should be lessened now as a result.

You can also use this approach for other negative futures. One fear many people have is of ageing. What is your negative thought? It might be 'I will be all alone when I am old.' That, in turn, could make you feel bad (about half of people are afraid of old age).[30] Now check what information this is based on. Do you know any old people that feel alone? Do you also know others that do not? Now do more research on old age. You might discover that most people get happier as they get older, not the other way around. Now review your assumptions: what are the beliefs that underpin your thought? It could be that beauty and fitness is what makes people happy. If so, ask yourself under what conditions you would change your mind. Now find an alternative future. You could go and follow people of the Ageist movement, which promotes and does research on healthy and happy ageing. Then write down everything we do not yet know about old age: progress in science and technology could make old age in the future a radically different one. Then reformulate: 'I will not be all alone when I am old if...' and identify action points. Go and work out, nurture your friendships—whatever you do, shape your future.

TROUBLESHOOTING

Let us take another pretty bad future many fear (again, after having forgotten about it for a while)—that of a nuclear holocaust. This is essentially the idea that the use of nuclear weapons will lead to the extinction of humanity (beginning to see a pattern here). Unsurprisingly, this thought strikes terror in people's hearts. Now, let us review where this idea comes from. You might realise you know very little about nuclear weapons, but you have heard that they are the worst weapon humans have. Now do more research. You will learn that the idea of human extinction through nuclear weapons is disputed[31]—this does not mean that they cannot kill many people, but that they cannot kill all of them. For instance, more than 650,000 Japanese survived the nuclear bombs of 1945. Make it as concrete as possible for yourself. You might discover that the world had many more nuclear weapons 20 years ago, or that they had not been used since 1945. Spell out the assumptions you have about nuclear weapons and when you would change them. Now research all the literature that explains not only why a nuclear holocaust is not likely but also why the use of a nuclear weapon is not. Reformulate: 'there won't be a nuclear war if...' Now, realise that you can literally do nothing as an individual about this particular future.

You have one option left: acceptance. Viktor Frankl, the famous holocaust survivor, invented the term 'tragic optimism' for this, meaning to maintain hope and find meaning in crisis. 'Man does not simply exist but always decides what his existence will be, what he will become the next moment. By the same token, every human being has the freedom to change at any instant.' If we cannot change this future, we need to accept it. Whether it's with meditation, stoicism, Buddhism, focus on what is in front of you. The future is not here. The now is. You will always have the choice of being in the present and deciding what you feel about it now.

5.4 *When we do not know what to fill the future with*

Sometimes, we simply have no idea what to do with our future.

Here you are—free from crisis, depression or fear, and still, you do not know what to make of your future. When you are young, this is a perfectly normal state to be in: we do not even have a fully-fledged concept of time until we are teenagers, let alone of the future as a space that we can shape. The question 'What do you want to be when you grow up?' therefore rarely gets a sophisticated or accurate answer. However, from young adulthood onwards, we feel the pressure to fill the future with something we are striving towards: we are asked to choose a career, a partner, a life path and stick to it!

For many of us, this is a daunting exercise. For one, the choice is wide. Whereas our ancestors had pretty much one life cut out for them—in one village, within one social class, sexual orientation and one job—we are (almost) free to choose where we want to live, what we want to do, who we want to love and how, and we are also free to choose over and over again. Thanks to urbanisation, social mobility, migration and industrialisation, we can start life out as the great-granddaughter of a cobbler from Slovenia and find ourselves with a PhD living in Rome. (Just for instance.) However, none of these possible choices come with a manual, and we are responsible for them.

As this freedom is daunting, most of us will go for the conventional future, choosing the one society expects from us. In sociology, you call this a cultural life script: the shared expectations about the order and timing of life events in an ordinary future.[32] We absorb them more or less as teenagers, which may also explain why we have no clear idea of a future before that age. In Western countries, these are more or less the same: education, career, property, marriage and children are regularly named as the most common life goals. People are not particularly original when it comes to smaller life goals either: 53% of Americans want to go on a wine tour in Napa, and 45% want to ride a hot air balloon and see the Northern Lights.[33]

Cultural life scripts are convenient as they give us the feeling that we are on track with our future, but they come with a few problems attached. The first is that they are not universal, even though they may look it. Life goals vary from country to country, from city to countryside, from social class to social class and of course from gender to gender.[34]

This brings us to the second problem with life scripts: societies differ considerably with regard to how much people's lives overlap with them. In other words, these life goals do not seem to be 'natural': they are socially constructed, and therefore, they can change if you want them to. (An idea confirmed by migrants whose life goals are influenced by the several cultures they are immersed in.)[35] In Denmark, 70% of people's futures are the ones that society tells them to have, but this is only the case for 46% of Americans (perhaps also because African Americans, in particular, disagree with common American life goals);[36] 45% of Americans and 49% of Brits are married, and 66% of Americans and 50% of Brits own their property; 84% of American women are mothers, and 82% of all British adults are parents. While marriage, house and children remain a feature in the future of many, they are by no means universal. Then, how do we read these numbers? If you trust the media, not complying with these life goals means failure (a word that is often used to describe the end of a relationship), but what if it just means somebody freely choosing their life goals?

The third problem with cultural life scripts is that they do not stretch out over life but are clustered in the 20s and 30s. As a result, we hit a wall (or a crisis) when we turn 40 or 50: from now on, society has no more futures for us—is life over? People think it is too late to learn a new language (not true, studies have shown)[37] or a new sport (not true, studies have shown),[38] or that it is all downhill cognitively (you guessed it: not true either).[39] A longitudinal Harvard study showed that no, it is never too late to change and evolve.[40] People continue to imagine futures for themselves all the way to the age of 80. Some biases are standing in our way of this. Not only are we not particularly creative, but we generally succumb to the status quo bias—a preference for things to remain the same.[41] We also suffer from self-limiting beliefs, meaning that we find reasons not to go for what we want. However, middle age defeatism is the price to pay when we go on autopilot with our futures and just integrate whatever society says we should want from our future.

Lastly, perhaps the most important problem with cultural life scripts as futures is that they do not necessarily make you happy. This might sound like a bumper sticker, but studies have shown that it will not be any of the boxes you will have checked, or any goal you have completed that will make your life a 'success'.[42] This brings us to a philosophical question: what is the purpose of having a future, of being able to imagine one, if not to guide us towards a good life? Which then begets the next question: what is a good life? A Harvard study tracked the same individuals for over 80 years and found that 'through all the years of studying these lives, one crucial factor stands out for the consistency and power of its ties to physical health, mental health, and longevity. Contrary to what many people might think, it's not career achievement, or exercise, or a healthy diet. Don't get us wrong; these things matter (a lot). But one thing continuously demonstrates its broad and enduring importance: Good relationships.'[43] It was not only this study that found this; others have confirmed that intrinsic goals, such as fulfilment from deep, enduring relationships, make us more satisfied than extrinsic goals such as earning money, owning stuff, and achieving reputation and fame.[44] Yet none of the societal futures are formulated along those lines. We are pressured towards a materialistic future of wanting and having rather than being and feeling.

Then, what does this mean for choosing your future(s)? It means not going on autopilot but choosing a sensual future of adjectives mindfully, over and over again. Choose how you want to feel: connected, fulfilled, wise, loved, appreciated.

At the risk of sounding new age-y, you need to be mindful about it and self-aware. For a lot of us this takes effort with the busyness of twenty-first-century life. Journaling, pausing, meditating and being bored are all ways to let the mind flow. Find out the difference between wanting and being. Do I want to be married or in a happy relationship? They are not the same, but to our newspapers, they are. Do I want to be rich or fulfilled? What is my life worth after my children grow up, after I have attained all those goals?

Be inspired. Look at the life goals of others. Learn from people with extraordinary life paths. Learn from older people. Go into nature. Grow. Create a vision board. Keep a diary. Find playfulness in it. Learn a new skill. Look at how far you have come. Give yourself time. Travel. No matter how many goals you check, you will never arrive because life is not a straight line but a loop, or a spiral where we constantly discover new futures.

6

YOUR FUTURE WARRANTY

You can't return a broken future, and money can't buy a beautiful one. In this sense, there is no guarantee in the classic sense, no right to the future as a product. There is, however, absolutely a right to keep inventing the future ourselves—both for us as individuals and for us as humanity as a whole. Because despite all the prophecies of doom, only one thing is certain: for us as individuals, death and for humanity, that the sun will go out in five billion years. Everything else has yet to be written.

This act of invention is the first step towards the future. Be it utopias or science fiction, the beginning is always made in the virtual, imaginary space that is the ultimate future. Historically, it is therefore no coincidence that the idea of a better future was born first, and only then did the implementation begin. Whether it was prosperity or equal rights for all, the discovery of America, the weather forecast, mobile phones or trips to the moon: everything started with an often derided idea.[1] Many of these ideas were highly successful: almost everything French author Jules Verne wrote in the nineteenth century (from submarines to television) now exists, which is why he is no longer considered a science fiction author by many.

Nevertheless, utopias or other proposed solutions for the future are often ridiculed, dismissed as dubious, as if they fail to recognise the seriousness of the situation. Especially when the present is particularly unpleasant, it is considered inappropriate to imagine a better future. However, utopias only arise in such circumstances precisely because they seek positive alternatives to the present, because they think through the answer to the question 'what if?' The future is not a static fact, but rather, the space of possibility that one repeatedly creates from it; it is the direct consequence of the idea that being human ultimately, anywhere and everywhere, means being more than the present.[2]

To deny oneself even the thought game with the future is actually irresponsible: first towards oneself, because people who think longer into the future are healthier, live longer and generally achieve their goals.[3] However, it is even more irresponsible towards future generations because if humanity does not die out in the next few years, as some people are predicting—without any basis, by the way—there will be 10,000 people for every one of us in the next million years. (Not all at the same time, of course.)[4] We have been living this idea of intergenerational fairness for centuries; without the dreams and ideas of our ancestors, we would not be where we are today, neither economically or legally, nor in terms of health. Defeatism, pessimism or even worse have not made today come true, but utopias or—for those for whom this word is too grandiose—new ideas.

These are everywhere—you just have to look for them. Proposals have been made to shorten the working week in order to improve productivity and reduce CO2 emissions (an idea already proposed by President Nixon, by the way); legislative proposals have suggested distributing the negative effects of climate change more fairly or to force governments to think long-term.[5] Everywhere, people are working feverishly on all kinds of futuristic technologies, be it superconductors that could revolutionise our power grids or fusion reactors. Research is being conducted into the latest drugs to combat cancer and Alzheimer's; devices are being designed to make it easier for disabled people to take part in everyday life; developments are being made in agriculture to use less water, and new technologies are helping to fish plastic out of the ocean and make many materials easier to recycle. Artificial intelligence can do jobs for us that we do not want to do ourselves anyway. We are developing an increasing number of methods to recognise disasters and crises earlier, both in the economy and in the environment. Some far-sighted people dream of eternal life or life on Mars,[6] and in philosophy, a growing movement sees humanity not just as a phenomenon of the last 5,000 years but as part of a long history and therefore also a long future. The trend towards the future is thus unbroken, but most of us are not paying attention.

The most important thing about our future capability is that we simply have to use it consciously. This does not mean that we should constantly be in the future in our minds, just as no entire Star Trek episode should be set in the holodeck, as the future is not a substitute for the present but an aid. This help should not be left on autopilot or bought from others, but it should be consciously switched on regularly, used and returned to the present with the knowledge gained. As individuals, symbolic moments such as New Year, birthdays or anniversaries are suitable—although New Years' resolutions are often ridiculed, you are actually twice as likely to keep them if you make them on such days. However, companies, political parties and even schools and civil associations should make time for the future once a year.[7]

We all have the ability to think about the future, that is the warranty. If you want to become particularly good at it, you should above all sharpen your mind, never give up, enjoy thinking, tolerate mistakes, have a certain sense of vitality, gain different experiences, read a lot, have energy, see yourself as a creative being, take risks and—last but not least—see change as a normal part of life.[8]

pp. [2–11]

NOTES

INTRODUCTION

1. Baumeister, R. F., et al. (2020). "Everyday Thoughts in Time: Experience Sampling Studies of Mental Time Travel." *Personality and Social Psychology Bulletin, 46*(12), 1631–1648. Tonn, B. E., et al. (2006). "Cognitive Representations of the Future: Survey Results." *Futures, 38,* 818.
2. Ji, L. J., et al. (2019). "Culture, Psychological Proximity to the Past and Future, and Self-Continuity." *European Journal of Social Psychology, 49*(4), 735–747. Ji, L. J., et al. (2008). "To Buy or to Sell: Cultural Differences in Stock Market Decisions Based on Price Trends." *Journal of Behavioral Decision Making, 21*(4), 399–413. Lam, K. C. H., et al. (2005). "Cultural Differences in Affective Forecasting: The Role of Focalism." *Personality and Social Psychology Bulletin, 31*(9), 1296–1309. https://doi.org/10.1177/0146167205274691
3. Luhmann, H.-J. (2001). *Die Blindheit der Gesellschaft: Filter der Risikowahrnehmung.* Gerling Akademie Verlag.
4. Our World in Data, "Countries that are democracies and autocracies in the world," https://ourworldindata.org/grapher/countries-democracies-autocracies-row?country=~OWID_WRL. Gapminder, "32 improvements," https://www.gapminder.org/factfulness-book/32-improvements/
5. Centre for the Future of Democracy, "Global Satisfaction with Democracy 2020," University of Cambridge, https://www.cam.ac.uk/system/files/report2020_003.pdf
6. Edelman Trust Barometer, "Unprepared for the Future," 2020, https://cdn2.hubspot.net/hubfs/440941/Trust%20Barometer%202020/2020%20Edelman%20Trust%20Barometer%20Global%20Report.

pdf?utm_campaign=Global:%20Trust%20Barometer%202020&utm_source=Website https://cdn2.hubspot.net/hubfs/440941/Trust%20Barometer%202020/2020%20Edelman%20Trust%20Barometer%20Global%20Report.pdf?utm_campaign=Global:%20Trust%20Barometer%202020&utm_source=Website

7. Pew Research Center, "Americans are more pessimistic than optimistic about many aspects of the country's future," 18 September 2023, https://www.pewresearch.org/short-reads/2023/09/18/americans-are-more-pessimistic-than-optimistic-about-many-aspects-of-the-countrys-future/

8. CNN, "Poll: Young Americans say they're fearful about the future of the country," 1 December 2021, https://edition.cnn.com/2021/12/01/politics/harvard-poll-young-americans/index.html

9. Ipsos, "Global advisor predictions 2023," https://www.ipsos.com/sites/default/files/ct/news/documents/2022-12/Ipsos%20Global%20Advisor%20Predictions%20Poll%20for%202023.pdf. Social Science Research Network, "Climate anxiety in children and young people and their beliefs about government responses to climate change: a global survey," September 2021, https://papers.ssrn.com/sol3/papers.cfm?abstract_id=3918955

10. Vox, "Cosmologist Martin Rees gives humanity a 50-50 chance of surviving the 21st century," 18 October 2018, https://www.vox.com/future-perfect/2018/10/18/17886974/science-technology-climate-change-existential-threats-martin-rees

11. McDonell, S., "Chinese people optimistic about the future, says Pew survey," BBC, October 2016, https://www.bbc.com/news/blogs-china-blog-37570965. Arab News, "Young Saudis optimistic about future, Arab Youth Survey shows," 1 May 2019, https://www.arabnews.com/node/1490621/saudi-arabia

12. Levada Center, "Assessments of social well-being in January 2023," February 2023, https://www.levada.ru/en/2023/02/16/assessments-of-social-well-being-in-january-2023/. "Visions of the future: planning horizon and attitudes," 14 February 2023, https://www.levada.ru/en/2023/02/14/visions-of-the-future-planning-horizon-and-attitudes/

13. Valdai Club, "The age of pandemic: year two. The future is back," 2021, https://valdaiclub.com/files/35821/

14. Levada Center, "Visions of the future: planning horizon and attitudes,"

February 2023, https://www.levada.ru/en/2023/02/14/visions-of-the-future-planning-horizon-and-attitudes/
15. Edelman, "Edelman Trust Barometer 2022," https://www.edelman.com/sites/g/files/aatuss191/files/2022-01/2022%20Edelman%20Trust%20Barometer%20FINAL_Jan25.pdf
16. McKinsey, "The case against corporate short termism," 4 August 2017, https://www.mckinsey.com/mgi/overview/in-the-news/the-case-against-corporate-short-termism
17. Lamm, H., et al. (1976). "Sex and Social Class as Determinants of Future Orientation (Time Perspective) in Adolescents." *Journal of Personality and Social Psychology*, *34*(3), 317–326.

1. TECHNICAL SPECIFICATIONS

1. Ulrich, R. (2012). "With the Past Behind and the Future Ahead: Back-to-front Representation of Past and Future Sentences." *Memory & Cognition*, *40*, 483–495.
2. Gilbert, D. T., & Wilson, T. D. (2007). "Prospection: Experiencing the Future." *Science*, *317*. Zentall, T. R. (2013). "Animals represent the past and the future." *Evolutionary Psychology*, *11*(3), 573–590.
3. Hernandez, W. A. (2016). "St. Augustine on Time." *International Journal of Humanities and Social Science*, *6*(6).
4. McTaggart, J. M. E. (1908). "The Unreality of Time." *Mind*, *17*, 457–474. Bittner, M. (2014). *Temporality: Universals and Variation*. Wiley-Blackwell.
5. Webb, R., "How to think about... Time," *New Scientist*, 27 June 2018, https://www.newscientist.com/article/mg23831840-400-how-to-think-about-time/
6. Rovelli, C. (2018). *The Order of Time*. Allen Lane.
7. Wearden, J. H., & Penton-Voak, I. S. (1995). "Feeling the Heat: Body Temperature and the Rate of Subjective Time, Revisited." *Quarterly Journal of Experimental Psychology*, *48*(2), 129–141. Zhong, C. B., & Devoe, S. E. (2010). "You Are How You Eat: Fast Food and Impatience." *Psychological Science*, *21*(5), 619–622.
8. Fayolle, S., et al. (2015). "Fear and Time: Fear Speeds Up the Internal Clock." *Behavioural Processes*, *120*, 135–140.
9. Buonomano, D. (2017). *Your Brain is a Time Machine: The Neuroscience and Physics of Time*. W. W. Norton & Company.

10. Rhemann, M. (2018). "Deepening Futures with Neuroscience." *World Futures Review*, *11*(1), 51–68.
11. Igarashi, K. M., et al. (2014). "Coordination of Entorhinal–Hippocampal Ensemble Activity during Associative Learning." *Nature*, *510*, 143–147. Miles, A. N., & Berntsen, D. (2011). "Odour-Induced Mental Time Travel into the Past and Future: Do Odour Cues Retain a Unique Link to Our Distant Past?" *Memory*, *19*(8), 930–940.
12. Science Daily, "Your brain on imagination: It's a lot like reality, study shows," 10 December 2018, https://www.sciencedaily.com/releases/2018/12/181210144943.htm
13. D'Argembeau A., et al. (2011). "Frequency, Characteristics and Functions of Future-Oriented Thoughts in Daily Life." *Applied Cognitive Psychology*, *25*, 96–103. Baumeister, R. (2016). "Pragmatic Prospection." In Seligman, M. E., et al. (eds), *Homo Prospectus*. Oxford University Press, 165.
14. Tulving, E. (1985). "Memory and Consciousness." *Canadian Psychological Association*, *26*(1), 1–12.
15. Seligman, M. E., et al. (2016). *Homo Prospectus*. Oxford University Press.
16. de Berker, A. O., et al. (2016). "Computations of Uncertainty Mediate Acute Stress Responses in Humans." *Nature Communications*, *7*(10996).
17. Burton, R. (2008). *On Being Certain: Believing You Are Right Even When You Are Wrong*. St. Martin's Press.
18. Gholipour, B., "A famous argument against free will has been debunked", *The Atlantic*, 10 September 2019, https://www.theatlantic.com/health/archive/2019/09/free-will-bereitschaftspotential/597736/
19. Baumeister, R. (2016). "Pragmatic Prospection." In Seligman, M. E., et al. (eds), *Homo Prospectus*, 159. Oxford University Press.
20. Sripada, C. (2016). "Free Will and the Construction of Options." In Seligman, M. E., et al. (eds), *Homo Prospectus*, 191–206. Oxford University Press.
21. Sharot, T. (2011). *The Optimism Bias: A Tour of the Irrationally Positive Brain*. Pantheon Books.
22. Farber, M. L. (1953). "Time Perspective and Feeling Tone: A Study in the Perception of Days." *Journal of Psychology*, *35*, 253–257.
23. Rasmussen, A. S., & Berntsen, D. (2013). "The Reality of the Past Versus the Ideality of the Future: Emotional Valence and Functional Differences between Past and Future Mental Time Travel." *Memory & Cognition*, *41*, 187–200.

24. Fischer, M., & Leitenberg, H. (1986). "Optimism and Pessimism in Elementary School-Aged Children." *Child Development*, *57*(1), 241–248.
25. Isaacowitz, D. M. (2005). "Correlates of Well-being in Adulthood and Old Age: A Tale of Two Optimisms." *Journal of Research in Personality*, *39*(2), 224–244.
26. Weinstein, N. D. (1980). "Unrealistic Optimism About Future Life Events." *Journal of Personality and Social Psychology*, *39*(5), 806–820.
27. Eyal, T., et al. (2004). "The Pros and Cons of Temporally Near and Distant Action." *Journal of Personality and Social Psychology*, *86*(6), 781–795.
28. Armor, D. A., et al. (2008). "Prescriptive Optimism: Is it Right to Be Wrong about the Future." *Psychological Science*, *19*, 329–333.
29. LiveScience, "Your brain 'shields' itself from the existential threat of death," 25 October 2019, https://www.livescience.com/brain-shields-idea-death.html
30. Sharot, T. (2011). *The Optimism Bias: A Tour of the Irrationally Positive Brain*. Pantheon/Random House.
31. Szpunar, K. K., & McDermott, K. B. (2008). "Episodic Future Thought and Its Relation to Remembering: Evidence from Ratings of Subjective Experience." *Consciousness and Cognition*, *17*, 330–334.
32. Rosa, H. (2005). *Beschleunigung: Die Veränderung der Zeitstrukturen in der Moderne*. Suhrkamp. 31–34.
33. Sheehy, G. (1976). *Passages: Predictable Life Crises of Adult Life*. Ballantine Books.
34. Kotre, J. (1995). "Generative Outcome." *Journal of Aging Studies*, *9*(1), 36.
35. Hoppmann, C. (2017). "Associations Among Individuals' Perceptions of Future Time, Individual Resources, and Subjective Well-Being in Old Age." *The Journal of Gerontology Series B*, *72*(3), 388–399.
36. Ettlin, F., & Hertwig, R. (2012). "Back or to the Future? Preferences of Time Travelers." *Judgment and Decision Making*, *7*(4), 373–382.
37. Siu, N. Y. F., et al. (2014). "Time Perception and Time Perspective Differences between Adolescents and Adults." *Acta Psychologica*, *151*, 222–229.
38. Sharot, T. (2011). *The Optimism Bias: A Tour of the Irrationally Positive Brain*. Pantheon Books.
39. Koselleck, R. (1979). *Vergangene Zukunft: Zur Semantik geschichtlicher Zeiten*. Suhrkamp.

40. Rosa, H. (2005). *Beschleunigung: Die Veränderung der Zeitstrukturen in der Moderne*, Suhrkamp, 31–34.
41. Pew Research Center, "Where Americans and Europeans agree—and differ—in the values they see as important," 16 October 2019, https://www.pewresearch.org/fact-tank/2019/10/16/where-americans-and-europeans-agree-and-differ-in-the-values-they-see-as-important/
42. Keller, J., "What makes Americans so optimistic? Why the U.S. tends to look on the bright side," *The Atlantic*, 25 March 2015, https://www.theatlantic.com/politics/archive/2015/03/the-american-ethic-and-the-spirit-of-optimism/388538/
43. Smith, C., & Davies, E. T. (2012). *Emigrating Beyond Earth: Human Adaptation and Space Colonization*. Springer. 25. Carter, B., & McCrea, W. H. (1983). "The Anthropic Principle and Its Implications for Biological Evolution." *Philosophical Transactions of the Royal Society of London, A310*(1512), 347–363. Gott III, J. R. (1993). "Implications of the Copernican Principle for Our Future Prospects." *Nature, 363*(6427), 315–319. Rees, M. (2018). *On the Future: Prospects for Humanity*. Princeton University Press.
44. Institute for the Future, "The American future gap," 13 April 2017, https://www.iftf.org/americanfuturegap/
45. Szpunar K. K., & McDermott, K. B. (2008). "Episodic Future Thought and Its Relation to Remembering: Evidence from Ratings of Subjective Experience." *Consciousness and Cognition*, *17*, 330–334.
46. Daniel Gilbert, "The psychology of your future self," TED Talk, March 2014, https://www.ted.com/talks/dan_gilbert_ the_psychology_of_your_future_self?language=en
47. Pronin, E. (2008). "Doing unto Future Selves as You Would Do unto Others: Psychological Distance and Decision Making." *Personality and Social Psychology Bulletin*, *34*(2), 224–236. Ersner-Hershfield, H., et al. (2009). "Saving for the Future Self: Neural Measures of Future Self-Continuity Predict Temporal Discounting." *Social Cognitive and Affective Neuroscience*, *4*(1), 85–92.
48. Rosa, H. (2005). *Beschleunigung: Die Veränderung der Zeitstrukturen in der Moderne,* Suhrkamp, 31–34.
49. Droit-Volet, S. (2013). "Time Perception in Children: A Neurodevelopmental Approach." *Neuropsychologia, 51*(2), 220–234. https://www.sciencedirect.com/science/article/abs/pii/S00 28393212003958
50. Wayman, Erin, "When did the human mind evolve to what it

is today?", *Smithsonian Magazine*, 25 June 2012, https://www.smithsonianmag.com/science-nature/when-did-the-human-mind-evolve-to-what-it-is-today-140507905/
51. Bottéro, J., & Bahrani, Z. (1992). *Mesopotamia: Writing, Reasoning, and the Gods*, pp. 125–137. The University of Chicago Press.
52. Annus, A. (ed.) (2010). *Divination and Interpretation of Signs in the Ancient World*. The Oriental Institute of the University of Chicago.
53. Cryer, F. H. (1994). *Divination in Ancient Israel and Its Near Eastern Environment: A Socio-historical Investigation*, 157. A&C Black. Rochberg, F. (2010). *Prayer, Magic, and the Stars in the Ancient and Late Antique World*, 169. Penn State Press. Winitzer, A. (2011). "Writing and Mesopotamian Divination: The Case of Alternative Interpretation." *Journal of Cuneiform Studies*, 63, 77–94. Annus, A. (ed.) (2010). *Divination and Interpretation of Signs in the Ancient World*. The Oriental Institute of the University of Chicago. Rochberg, F. (2010). *In the Path of the Moon: Babylonian Celestial Divination and Its Legacy*. Brill. 304.
54. Holden, J. (1996). *A History of Horoscopic Astrology*. American Federation of Astrologers.
55. Cicero, M. T., *De Divinatione*. Santangelo, F. (2013). *Divination, Prediction and the End of the Roman Republic*. Cambridge University Press.
56. Jewish Encyclopedia, "Eschatology," https://www.jewishencyclopedia.com/articles/5849-eschatology
57. Calvin, J. (1960). "Institutes of the Christian Religion." In McNeill, J. T. (ed., trans). *Ford Lewis Battles*. 3.21.5. Westminster Press.
58. Hulswit, M. (1980). "A short history of 'causation,'" http://see.library.utoronto.ca/SEED/Vol4-3/Hulswit.htm. Mackie, J. L. (1980). *The Cement of the Universe: A Study of Causation*. Oxford University Press.

2. THE FUNCTIONS OF EACH PART

1. Morsella, E., et al. (2010). "The Spontaneous Thoughts of the Night: How Future Tasks Breed Intrusive Cognitions." *Social Cognition*, 28(5), 641–650.
2. Kaufman, S. B., & Singer, J. L. "The origins of positive-constructive daydreaming." *Scientific American*, 22 December 2011, https://blogs.scientificamerican.com/guest-blog/the-origins-of-positive-constructive-daydreaming/
3. Godwin, C. A., et al. (2017). "Functional Connectivity Within and

Between Intrinsic Brain Networks Correlates with Trait Mind Wandering." *Neuropsychologia*, *103*, 140–153.
4. Bench, S. W., & Lench, H. C. (2013). "On the Function of Boredom," *Behavioural Sciences*, *3*, 459–472.
5. Popper, R. (2008). "Foresight Methodology." In Georghiou, L., et al. (eds), *The Handbook of Technology Foresight*. Edward Elgar. 44–88. Schwartz, P. (1996). *The Art of the Long View: Planning for the Future in an Uncertain World*, 29–43. Currency Doubleday.
6. Wilkinson, A., & Kupers, R. (2013). "Living in the Futures." *Harvard Business Review, 91*(5), 118–127.
7. Sripada, C. (2016). "Imaginative Guidance: A Mind Forever Wandering." In Seligman, M. E., et al. (eds), *Homo Prospectus*, 105. Oxford University Press.
8. Grossmann, G. (1953). "Der Elementare Teil der Grossmann-Methode. Stufe 1: Das Glückstagebuch oder Einführung in die Methodische Zeitplanung. München 1953 [The Basics of the Grossmann-Method. Step 1: The Happy Day Planner or Introduction to Methodical Time Planning]." In Grossmann, G. (ed.), *Die Originaleinführung der „Grossmann-Methode", HelfRecht—Studienzentrum GmbH* (Hrsg.) (Bad Alexandersbad: HelfRecht-Studienzentrum GmbH, 1983), 227–414.
9. Locke, E. A. (1968). "Toward a Theory of Task Motivation and Incentives." *Organizational Behavior and Human Performance*, *3*(2), 157–189.
10. Locke, E. A., et al. (1981). "Goal Setting and Task Performance: 1969–1980." *Psychological Bulletin*, *90*(1), 125–152.
11. Dalton, A. N., & Stephen, A. S. (2012). "Too Much of a Good Thing: The Benefits of Implementation Intentions Depend on the Number of Goals." *Journal of Consumer Research*, *39*(3).
12. Carnegie Mellon University, "New research finds the time of day when a student takes a class can affect the major selected later in the academic career," 23 January 2020, https://www.cmu.edu/news/stories/archives/2020/january/major-decisions.html
13. Nan, X., & Qin, Y. (2019). "How Thinking about the Future Affects Our Decisions in the Present: Effects of Time Orientation and Episodic Future Thinking on Responses to Health Warning Messages." *Human Communication Research*, *45*(2), 148–168.
14. Strathman, A., et al. (1994). "The Consideration of Future Consequences Scale: Weighing Immediate and Distant Outcomes of Behavior." *Journal of Personality and Social Psychology*, *66*, 742–752. Bickel, W. K., et al. (2014).

"The Behavioral- and Neuro-economic Process of Temporal Discounting: A Candidate Behavioral Marker of Addiction." *Neuropharmacology, 76*(Pt B), 518–527. Chapman, G. B. (1996). "Temporal Discounting and Utility for Health and Money." *Journal of Experimental Psychology: Learning, Memory, and Cognition, 22,* 771–791. Chapman, G. B. (1998). "Sooner or Later: The Psychology of Intertemporal Choice. In Medin, D. L. (ed.), *The Psychology of Learning and Motivation*, v. 38, 83–113. Academic Press. Orbell, S., & Kyriakaki, M. (2008). "Temporal Framing and Persuasion to Adopt Preventive Health Behavior: Moderating Effects of Individual Differences in Consideration of Future Consequences on Sunscreen Use." *Health Psychology, 27,* 770–779. Barlow, P., et al. (2017). "Time-Discounting and Tobacco Smoking: A Systematic Review and Network Analysis." *International Journal of Epidemiology, 46*(3), 860–869.
15. Ji, L. J., et al. (2019). "Culture, Psychological Proximity to the Past and Future, and Self-Continuity." *European Journal of Social Psychology, 49*(4), 735–747. Ji, L. J., et al. (2008). "To Buy or to Sell: Cultural Differences in Stock Market Decisions based on Stock Price Trends." *Journal of Behavioral Decision Making, 21*(4), 399–413. Lam, K. C. H., et al. (2005). "Cultural Differences in Affective Forecasting: The Role of Focalism." *Personality and Social Psychology Bulletin, 31*(9), 1296–1309.
16. Mischel, W., et al. (1989). "Delay of Gratification in Children." *Science, 244*(4907), 933–938.
17. Kidda, C., et al. (2013). "Rational Snacking: Young Children's Decision-Making on the Marshmallow Task Is Moderated by Beliefs about Environmental Reliability." *Cognition, 126*(1), 109–114.
18. Jacquet, J., et al. (2013). "Intra- and Intergenerational Discounting in the Climate Game." *Nature Climate Change, 3,* 125–128.
19. Zaval, L., et al. (2014). "How Warm Days Increase Belief in Global Warming." *Nature Climate Change, 4,* 143–147.
20. Woodzicka, J. A., & LaFrance, M. (2001). "Real Versus Imagined Gender Harassment." *Journal of Social Issues, 57*(1), 15–30. Ayton, P., et al. (2007). "Affective Forecasting: Why Can't People Predict Their Emotions?" *Thinking & Reasoning, 13*(1), 62–80.
21. Loewenstein, G., et al. (2003). "Projection Bias in Predicting Future Utility." *Quarterly Journal of Economics, 118*(4), 1209–1248.
22. Samuelson, W., & Zeckhauser, R. (1988). "Status Quo Bias in Decision Making." *Journal of Risk and Uncertainty, 1,* 7–59.
23. Zimbardo, P., & Boyd, J. (1999). "Putting Time in Perspective: A Valid,

Reliable Individual-Differences Metric." *Journal of Personality and Social Psychology, 77*(6), 1271–1288.

24. Miloyan, B., et al. (2019). "Measuring Mental Time Travel: Is the Hippocampus Really Critical for Episodic Memory and Episodic Foresight?" *Cortex, 117,* 371–384.

25. Tulving, E. (1985). "Memory and Consciousness." *Canadian Journal of Psychology, 26,* 1–2. Khamsi, R., "Amnesiacs struggle to imagine future events," *New Scientist,* 15 January 2007, https://www.newscientist.com/article/dn10950-amnesiacs-struggle-to-imagine-future-events/#ixzz6sgrj6i9G

26. Barraza, J. A., et al. (2015). "The Heart of the Story: Peripheral Physiology During Narrative Exposure Predicts Charitable Giving." *Biological Psychology, 105,* 138–143.

27. Zak, P. J. (2014). "Why Your Brain Loves Good Storytelling." *Harvard Business Review, 28,* 1–5.

28. Wituschek, J., "Brand loyalty for Apple has hit an all-time high", Imore, 16 March 2021, https://www.imore.com/brand-loyalty-apple-has-hit-all-time-high. Ehrenberg, A. S. C. (1988). *Repeat-Buying: Facts, Theory and Application,* 16. Oxford University Press.

29. Baird, B., et al. (2011). "Back to the Future: Autobiographical Planning and the Functionality of Mind-Wandering." *Consciousness and Cognition, 20*(4), 1604–1611.

30. Neustadt, R. E., & May, E. R. (1986). *Thinking in Time: The Uses of History for Decision-Makers,* 44–52. The Free Press.

31. Khon, Y. F. (1992). *Analogies at War: Korea, Munich, Dien Bien Phu, and the Vietnam Decisions of 1965,* pp. 3–10. Princeton University Press. Tertrais, B. (2019). *La Revanche de l'Histoire.* Odile Jacob.

32. Neisser, U., & Harsch, N. (1992). "Phantom Flashbulbs: False Recollections of Hearing the News about Challenger." In Winograd, E. & Neisser, U. (eds), *Emory Symposia in Cognition, 4. Affect and Accuracy in Recall: Studies of "Flashbulb" Memories.* Cambridge University Press, 9–31. Hirst, W., et al. (2009). "Long-Term Memory for the Terrorist Attack of September 11: Flashbulb Memories, Event Memories, and the Factors that Influence their Retention." *Journal of Experimental Psychology, General, 138*(2), 161–176.

33. Odinot, G., et al. (2009). "Eyewitness Memory of a Supermarket Robbery: A Case Study of Accuracy and Confidence after 3 Months." *Law and Human Behavior, 33*(6), 506–514.

34. Price, N., et al. (2019). "Viking Warrior Women? Reassessing Birka Chamber Grave Bj.581." *Antiquity, 93*(367), 181–198.

35. Banner, J. M. (2021). *The Ever-Changing Past: Why All History is Revisionist History*, 239–250. Yale University Press.
36. Turchin, P. (2008). "Arise 'Cliodynamics.'" *Nature*, *454*(7200), 34–35.
37. Cambridge Dictionary, "Creativity", https://dictionary.cambridge.org/dictionary/english/creativity
38. Jung, R. E. (2015). "Quantity Yields Quality When It Comes to Creativity: A Brain and Behavioral Test of the Equal-Odds Rule." *Frontiers in Psychology, 6*, 864.
39. Green, E., "Innovation: The History of a Buzzword," *The Atlantic*, 20 June 2013, https://www.theatlantic.com/business/archive/2013/06/innovation-the-history-of-a-buzzword/277067/
40. Asimov, I., & Coté, J.-M. (1986). *Future Days: A Nineteenth-Century Vision of the Year 2000*. Virgin Books.
41. Madore, K. P. (2016). "Divergent Creative Thinking in Young and Older Adults: Extending the Effects of an Episodic Specificity Induction." *Memory & Cognition*, *44*(6), 974–988.
42. Seligman, M. E., et al. (2016). "Creativity and Aging: What We Can Make with What We Have Left." In Seligman, M. E., et al. (eds) *Homo Prospectus,* 305–350. Oxford University Press.
43. Ritter, S. M., et al. (2012). "Diversifying Experiences Enhance Cognitive Flexibility." *Journal of Experimental Social Psychology*, *48*(4), 961–964.
44. Tetlock, P. E., & Gardner, D. (2015). *Superforecasting: The Art and Science of Prediction,* 74. Crown Publishers.
45. Sternberg, R. J., & Frensch, P. A. (1992). "On Being an Expert: A Cost-Benefit Analysis." In Hoffman, R. R. (ed.), *The Psychology of Expertise,* 191–203. Springer.
46. D'Argembeau, A., & Van der Linden, M. (2006). "Individual Differences in the Phenomenology of Mental Time Travel: The Effect of Vivid Visual Imagery and Emotion Regulation Strategies." *Consciousness & Cognition*, *15*, 342–350.
47. Davies, C., & Sarpong, D. (2013). "The Epistemological Relevance of the Arts in Foresight and Future Studies." *Futures*, *47*, 1–8.
48. Harmon-Jones, E., et al. (2013). "Does Negative Affect Always Narrow and Positive Affect Always Broaden the Mind? Considering the Influence of Motivational Intensity on Cognitive Scope." *Current Directions in Psychological Science, 22*(4), 301–307. Ceci, M. W., & Kumar, V. K. (2016). "A Correlational Study of Creativity, Happiness, Motivation, and Stress from Creative Pursuits." *Journal of Happiness Studies*, *17*, 609–626.

49. Walker, M. (2017). *Why We Sleep: The New Science of Sleep and Dreams*, 132. Penguin Books.
50. Sorrentino, R. M., et al. (1992). "Uncertainty Orientation." In Smith, C. (ed.), *Motivation and Personality: Handbook of Thematic Content Analysis*, 419–427. Cambridge University Press.
51. Nan, X., & Qin, Y. (2019). "How Thinking about the Future Affects Our Decisions in the Present: Effects of Time Orientation and Episodic Future Thinking on Responses to Health Warning Messages." *Human Communication Research, 45*(2), 148–168.

3. HOW TO USE IT

1. Eisenstein, M., "What's your risk of catching COVID? These tools help you to find out," *Nature*, 21 December 2020, https://www.nature.com/articles/d41586-020-03637-y
2. Kiersz, A., "This is when you're going to die," *Business Insider*, 21 March 2014, https://www.businessinsider.com/social-security-life-table-charts-2014-3?r=US&IR=T
3. Wiston, M., & Mphale, K. M. (2018). "Weather Forecasting: From the Early Weather Wizards to Modern-day Weather Predictions." *Journal of Climatology & Weather Forecasting, 6*(2), 1–9.
4. National Oceanic and Atmospheric Administration, "How reliable are weather forecasts?", https://scijinks.gov/forecast-reliability/
5. Wilkins, A. "Earthquakes seem to come in a more predictable pattern than we thought," *New Scientist*, 23 August 2022, https://www.newscientist.com/article/2334746-earthquakes-seem-to-come-in-a-more-predictable-pattern-than-we-thought/
6. Rotaru, V., et al, "Event-level prediction of urban crime reveals a signature of enforcement bias in US cities", *Nature*, 30 June 2022, https://www.nature.com/articles/s41562-022-01372-0
7. van Eerde, W., & Azar, S. (2019). "Too Late? What Do You Mean? Cultural Norms Regarding Lateness for Meetings and Appointments." *Cross-Cultural Research, 54*(2/3), 111–129.
8. Thompson, E. P. (1967). "Time, Work-Discipline, and Industrial Capitalism." *Past & Present, 38*, 56–97.
9. Office of Rail and Road, "Passenger rail performance, 2020—2021, Quarter 4", May 2021, https://dataportal.orr.gov.uk/statistics/performance/passenger-rail-performance/. Déléaz, T., "Retards, fréquentation, trains supprimés... Quel bilan pour la SNCF en 2018", *Le Point*, August 2019,

https://www.lepoint.fr/societe/sncf-pres-de-400-000-trains-ont-ete-supprimes-en-2018--16-08-2019-2330123_23.php
10. Orzel, C. (2022). *A Brief History of Timekeeping: The Science of Marking Time, from Stonehenge to Atomic Clocks,* 181–196. Oneworld.
11. Dolnick, E. (2017). *The Seeds of Life: From Aristotle to da Vinci, from Sharks' Teeth to Frogs' Pants, the Long and Strange Quest to Discover Where Babies Come From*. Basic Books.
12. Ortiz-Ospina, E., "Trust," Our World in Data, https://ourworldindata.org/trust
13. Feinstein, J. S., et al. (2011). "The Human Amygdala and the Induction and Experience of Fear." *Current Biology*, *21*(1), 34–38. Tranel, D., et al. (2006). "Altered Experience of Emotion Following Bilateral Amygdala Damage." *Cognitive Neuropsychiatry*, *11*, 219–232.
14. Beck, A. T., & Emery, G. (1985). *Anxiety Disorders and Phobias: A Cognitive Perspective,* p. 10. Basic Books.
15. "Hofstede: Uncertainty Avoidance Traits," https://www.andrews.edu/~tidwell/bsad560/HofstedeUncertainityAvoidance.html
16. Slovic, P. (2000). *The Perception of Risk*. Routledge.
17. Knight, F. H. (1921). *Risk, Uncertainty and Profit*. Houghton Mifflin Company.
18. Gardner, D. (2009). *The Science of Fear: How the Culture of Fear Manipulates Your Brain,* 65–66. Plume.
19. Spiegelhalter, D. (2019). *The Art of Statistics: Learning from Data,* pp. 205–228. Penguin Books.
20. Knight, F. H. (1940). "'What is Truth' in Economics?" *Journal of Political Economy*, *48*(1), 1–32.
21. WHO, "World Bank and WHO: Half the world lacks access to essential health services, 100 million still pushed into extreme poverty because of health expenses," 2017, https://www.who.int/news/item/13-12-2017-world-bank-and-who-half-the-world-lacks-access-to-essential-health-services-100-million-still-pushed-into-extreme-poverty-because-of-health-expenses
22. Kessler, D. et al. (2016). "The Macroeconomic Role of Insurance." In Hufeld, F., et al. (eds), *The Economics, Regulation, and Systemic Risk of Insurance Markets*. Oxford University Press. Lin, J., & Wang, D. (2015). "A Review on the Society Impact of Insurance." *Insurance Study* (in Chinese), 98–105.
23. Isidore, C., "This family lost their home in the Texas floods. Like most victims of storm, they didn't have flood insurance," CNN, 10 July

2025, https://edition.cnn.com/2025/07/10/business/texas-flooding-victims-lack-flood-insurance

24. Centers for Disease Control and Prevention, "Lifestyle risk factors," https://www.cdc.gov/environmental-health-tracking/php/data-research/lifestyle-risk-factors.html
25. Arms Control Association, "Nuclear weapons: who has what at a glance," January 2022, https://www.armscontrol.org/factsheets/Nuclearweaponswhohaswhat
26. Samuelson, W., & Zeckhauser, R. (1988). "Status Quo Bias in Decision Making." *Journal of Risk and Uncertainty*, *1*(1), 7–59.
27. Servier, J. (1967). *Histoire de l'Utopie,* pp. 15–26. Gallimard.
28. Bloch, E. (1959). *Das Prinzip Hoffnung*, Vol. I, 258. Suhrkamp.
29. Costa, V. D., et al. (2014). "Dopamine Modulates Novelty Seeking Behavior During Decision Making." *Behavioural Neuroscience, 128*(5), 556–566.
30. Baudin, L. (1928). *L'Empire Socialiste des Inca*, 65. Institut d'Ethnologie.
31. Bloch, E. (1959). *Das Prinzip Hoffnung*, Vol. I, 285. Suhrkamp.
32. Ibid., 278.
33. Servier, J. (1967). *Histoire de l'Utopie,* 323. Gallimard.
34. Rosling, H., et al. (2018). *Factfulness: Ten Reasons We're Wrong About the World—and Why Things Are Better Than You Think*. Flatiron Books.
35. Maese, R., "For Olympians, seeing (in their minds) is believing (it can happen)," 28 July 2016, *The Washington Post*, https://www.washingtonpost.com/sports/olympics/for-olympians-seeing-in-their-minds-is-believing-it-can-happen/2016/07/28/6966709c-532e-11e6-bbf5-957ad17b4385_story.html
36. Sharot, T. (2011). *The Optimism Bias: A Tour of the Irrationally Positive Brain*. Pantheon/Random House.
37. Lee, L. O., et al. (2019). "Optimism is Associated with Exceptional Longevity in 2 Epidemiologic Cohorts of Men and Women." *PNAS*, *116*(37), 18357–18362.
38. New York Public Radio, "Surprise! Why the unexpected feels good, and why it's good for us," 1 April 2015, https://www.wnyc.org/story/surprise-unexpected-why-it-feels-good-and-why-its-good-us/
39. Schultz, W. (1998). "Predictive Reward Signal of Dopamine Neurons." *Journal of Neurophysiology*, *80*(1), 1–27.
40. Mellers, B. A., et al. (2016). "Decision Affect Theory: Emotional Reactions to the Outcomes of Risky Options", *Psychological Science*, *8*(6), 423–429.

41. Renninger, L. A., & Luna, T. (2015). *Surprise: Embrace the Unpredictable and Engineer the Unexpected*. Penguin Publishing Group.
42. Gaub, F., & Boswinkel, L. (2020). "Who's First Wins? International Crisis Response to COVID-19." *EU Institute for Security Studies*, Brief 11. https://www.iss.europa.eu/content/who%E2%80% 99s-first-wins-international-crisis-response-covid-19#_introduction
43. Wirtz, J. J. (2003). "Theory of Surprise." In Betts, R. K., & Mahnken, T. (eds), *Paradoxes of Strategic Intelligence*. Routledge. Luttwak, E. (1987). *Strategy: The Logic of War and Peace,* 8. Harvard University Press.
44. Antony, J. W., et al. (2021). "Behavioral, Physiological, and Neural Signatures of Surprise during Naturalistic Sports Viewing." *Neuron*, *109*(2), 377–390. https://www.sciencedirect.com/science/article/pii/S0896627320308539
45. Brickman, P., et al. (1978). "Lottery winners and accident victims: is happiness relative?" *Journal of Personality and Social Psychology*, *36*(8), 917–927.
46. Merton, R., & Barber, E. (2004). *The Travels and Adventures of Serendipity: A Study in Historical Semantics and the Sociology of Science*. Princeton University Press.
47. Taleb, N. N. (2007). *The Black Swan: The Impact of the Highly Improbable*. Penguin.
48. Meissner, P., & Wulf, T. (2013). "Cognitive Benefits of Scenario Planning: Its Impact on Biases and Decision Quality." *Technological Forecasting and Social Change*, *80*(4), 801–814.
49. Betts, R. (1982). *Surprise Attack: Lessons for Defence Planning*. Brookings Institutions Press.
50. Ikani, N., & Meyer, C. O. (2022). "The Underlying Causes of Strategic Surprise in EU Foreign Policy: A Post-Mortem Investigation of the Arab Uprisings and the Ukraine–Russia Crisis of 2013/14," *European Security*. Grabo, C. (2010). *Handbook of Warning Intelligence: Assessing the Threat to National Security*. Scarecrow Press.
51. European Union External Action Service, "EU Ambassadors Annual Conference 2022: Opening speech by High Representative Josep Borrell," 10 October 2022, https://www.eeas.europa.eu/eeas/eu-ambassadors-annual-conference-2022-opening-speech-high-representative-josep-borrell_en. Goar, M., "'Qui aurait pu prédire la crise climatique?': Macron accusé de 'déconnexion' sur l'écologie," *Le Monde*, 3 January 2023, https://www.lemonde.fr/politique/article/2023/01/03/emmanuel-macron-et-le-climat-

un-discours-qui-rate-sa-cible_6156389_823448.html. Berkowitz, B. (2007). "U.S. Intelligence Estimates of Soviet Collapse: Reality and Perception." In Fukuyama, F. (ed.), *Blindsided: How to Anticipate Forcing Events and Wild Cards in Global Politics*, 29–41. Brookings Institution Press.

4. SAFETY INSTRUCTIONS

1. Loewenstein, G., et al. (2001). "Risk as Feelings." *Psychological Bulletin*, *127*(2), 267–286.
2. Gardner, D. (2008). *The Science of Fear: How the Culture of Fear Manipulates Your Brain,* 10. Plume.
3. Nowrasteh, A. "Fatalities and the annual chance of being murdered in a European terrorist attack," CATO Institute, 21 June 2017, https://www.cato.org/blog/european-terrorism-fatalities-annual-chance-being-murdered
4. Injury Facts, "Preventable deaths," https://injuryfacts.nsc.org/all-injuries/preventable-death-overview/odds-of-dying/. World Health Organisation, "Risk of premature death from the four target NCDs Data by WHO Region," https://apps.who.int/gho/data/view.main.2485REG?lang=en
5. *The Economist*, "Danger of death! How you are unlikely to die," 14 February 2013, https://www.economist.com/graphic-detail/2013/02/14/danger-of-death?fsrc=scn%2Ftw%2Fte%2Fdc%2Fdangerofdeath%20. Caesar, S., "NASA satellite plunges to Earth," *Los Angeles Times*, 24 September 2011, https://www.latimes.com/world/la-xpm-2011-sep-24-la-na-nasa-satellite-20110925-story.html
6. Perkins, C. A., "Age Patterns of Victims of Serious Violent Crime", https://bjs.ojp.gov/content/pub/pdf/apvsvc.pdf
7. McCarthy, J., "52% Describe Problem of Crime in the U.S. as Serious," Gallup, 13 November 2019, https://news.gallup.com/poll/268283/describe-problem-crime-serious.aspx
8. Kahneman, D. (2017). *Thinking, Fast and Slow,* 324. Penguin Books. World Economic Forum, "Most people around the world are overly pessimistic," December 2017, https://www.weforum.org/agenda/2017/12/you're-probably-too-pessimistic/
9. Fabio, R. A., & Suriano, R. (2021). "The Influence of Media Exposure on Anxiety and Working Memory during Lockdown Period in Italy." *International Journal for Environmental Research and Public Health*, *18*(17), 9279. Prieto Curiel, R., et al. (2020). "Crime and Its Fear in Social Media." *Palgrave Communications*, *6*(57). Pew Research Center,

"War Coverage," https://www.pewresearch.org/journalism/2002/05/23/war-coverage/
10. Pfefferbaum, B. (2014). "Disaster Media Coverage and Psychological Outcomes: Descriptive Findings in the Extant Research." *Current Psychiatry Reports*, *16*(464). Rozado, D., et al. (2022). "Longitudinal Analysis of Sentiment and Emotion in News Media Headlines Using Automated Labelling with Transformer Language Models." *PLoS ONE 17*(10), e0276367.
11. McLean, C. P., et al. (2011). "Gender Differences in Anxiety Disorders: Prevalence, Course of Illness, Comorbidity and Burden of Illness." *Journal of Psychiatric Research*, *45*(8), 1027–1035. National Institute of Mental Health, "Any Anxiety Disorder," https://www.nimh.nih.gov/health/statistics/any-anxiety-disorder. Chang, E. C., et al. (2001). "Cultural Variations in Optimistic and Pessimistic Bias: Do Easterners Really Expect the Worst and Westerners Really Expect the Best When Predicting Future Life Events?" *Journal of Personality and Social Psychology*, *81*(3), 476–491.
12. Whitfield, J. B., et al. (2020). "Pessimism Is Associated with Greater All-Cause and Cardiovascular Mortality, but Optimism Is Not Protective." *Scientific Reports*, *10*(12609).
13. France, C. R., et al. (2020). "Pain Resilience and Catastrophizing Combine to Predict Functional Restoration Program Outcomes." *Health Psychology*, *39*(7), 573–579.
14. Gellatly, R., & Beck, A. T. (2016). "Catastrophic Thinking: A Transdiagnostic Process Across Psychiatric Disorders", *Cognitive Therapy and Research*, *40*, 441–452.
15. Hazan, C., & Shave, P. (1987). "Romantic Love Conceptualized as an Attachment Process." *Journal of Personality and Social Psychology, 52*(3), 511–524.
16. Beck, A. T., & Emery, G. (1985). *Anxiety Disorders and Phobias: A Cognitive Perspective*, 23. Basic Books.
17. Wilson, J., "Boy Scout found after four days in Utah wilderness," *The Guardian*, 23 June 2005, https://www.theguardian.com/world/2005/jun/23/usa.jamiewilson
18. Blalock, G., et al. (2009). "Driving Fatalities After 9/11: A Hidden Cost of Terrorism." *Applied Economics*, *41*(14), 1717–1729.
19. Pierre, J. M. (2019). "The Psychology of Guns: Risk, Fear, and Motivated Reasoning." *Palgrave Communications*, *5*(159). Hemenway, D. (2011).

"Risks and Benefits of a Gun in the Home." *American Journal of Lifestyle Medicine,* 5(6).

20. Duncan, P., "Europeans greatly overestimate Muslim population, poll shows," *The Guardian,* 13 December 2016, https://www.theguardian.com/society/datablog/2016/dec/13/europeans-massively-overestimate-muslim-population-poll-shows

21. Feng, J., "More than 4 in 5 Russians fear nuclear war with U.S.—Poll," *Newsweek,* 21 April 2022, https://www.newsweek.com/ukraine-invasion-us-russia-china-nuclear-cold-war-1699626

22. Investopedia, "The lottery: Is it ever worth playing?", 6 January 2023, https://www.investopedia.com/managing-wealth/worth-playing-lottery/#:~:text=For%20example%2C%20the%20odds%20of,bee%20sting%20during%20your%20lifetime

23. Koenig, B. L., et al. (2007). "Misperception of Sexual and Romantic Interests in Opposite-Sex Friendships: Four Hypotheses." *Personal Relationships, 14,* 411–429. Perilloux, C., et al. (2012). "The Misperception of Sexual Interest." *Psychological Science,* 23(2), 146–151. Treat, T. A., et al. (2016). "Enhancing the Accuracy of Men's Perceptions of Women's Sexual Interest in the Laboratory." *Psychology of Violence,* 6(4), 562.

24. Mayraz, G. (May 2013). "Wishful Thinking." The University of Melbourne, Department of Economics, Working Paper Series.

25. Wann, D. L., & Dolan, T. J. (1994). "Influence of Spectator's Identification on Evaluation of the Past, Present, and Future Performance of a Sports Team." *Perceptual and Motor Skills, 78,* 547–552. Babad, E., & Katz, Y. (1991). "Wishful Thinking—Against All Odds." *Journal of Applied Social Psychology 21*(23), 1921–1938.

26. Dolan, K.A., & Holbrook, T.M. (2001). "Knowing Versus Caring: The Role of Affect and Cognition in Political Perceptions." *Political Psychology, 22,* 27–44. Babad, E. (1997). "Wishful Thinking among Voters: Motivational and Cognitive Influences." *International Journal of Public Opinion Research, 9,* 105–125. Granberg, D., & Brent, E. (1983). "When Prophecy Bends: The Preference-Expectation Link in U.S. Presidential Elections, 1952–1980." *Journal of Personality and Social Psychology, 45,* 477–491. Meffert, M. F. (2011). "More than Wishful Thinking: Causes and Consequences of Voters' Electoral Expectations about Parties and Coalitions." *Electoral Studies,* 30(4), 804–815. Stiers, D., & Dassonneville, R. (2018). "Affect Versus Cognition: Wishful Thinking on Election Day:

An Analysis Using Exit Poll Data from Belgium." *International Journal of Forecasting*, *34*(2), 199–215.
27. Krizan, Z., et al. (2010). "Wishful Thinking in the 2008 U.S. Presidential Election." *Psychological Science, 21*(1), 140–146.
28. Orwell, G. (1945). "London Letter." *Partisan Review, 12*, 467–472.
29. Caplin, A., & Leahy, J. V. (2019). "Wishful Thinking." No. w25707, National Bureau of Economic Research. Reinhart, C. M., & Rogoff, K. S. (2011). *This Time Is Different: Eight Centuries of Financial Folly*. Princeton University Press.
30. Wucker, M. (2016). *The Gray Rhino: How to Recognize and Act on the Obvious Dangers We Ignore*. St. Martin's Press. YouTube, "Elon Musk motivation—wishful thinking (don't do it!)," https://www.youtube.com/watch?v=zXxD9pkK5fk
31. Tur-Sinai, A., et al. (2020). "The Accuracy of Self-Reported Dwelling Valuation." *Journal of Housing Economics*, *48*(101660).
32. Sigall, H., et al. (2000). "Wishful Thinking and Procrastination." *Journal of Social Behavior & Personality, 15*(5), 283–296.
33. Kahneman, D., & Tversky, A. (1977). "Intuitive Prediction: Biases and Corrective Procedures." DARPA Technical Report PTR-1042-7746. Buehler, R., et al. (2002). "Inside the Planning Fallacy: The Causes and Consequences of Optimistic Time Predictions." In Gilovich, T., et al. (eds), *Heuristics and Biases: The Psychology of Intuitive Judgment*, pp. 250–270. Cambridge University Press. Peetz, J. (2010). "Planning for the Near and Distant Future: How Does Temporal Distance Affect Task Completion Predictions?" *Journal of Experimental Social Psychology, 46*(5), 709–772.
34. Wucker, M. (2016). *The Gray Rhino: How to Recognize and Act on the Obvious Dangers We Ignore*. St. Martin's Press.
35. Munich Re, "Volcanic eruptions: The earth's ring of fire," https://www.munichre.com/en/risks/natural-disasters-losses-are-trending-upwards/volcanic-eruptions-the-earths-ring-of-fire.html. De Natale, G. (2020), "Invited Perspectives: The Volcanoes of Naples: How Can the Highest Volcanic Risk in the World Be Effectively Mitigated?" *Natural Hazards and Earth System Sciences, 20*(7), 2037–2053.
36. Navar, A. M., et al. (2021). "Patient-Perceived Versus Actual Risk of Cardiovascular Disease and Associated Willingness to Consider and Use Prevention Therapy." *Circulation: Cardiovascular Quality and Outcomes, 14*(1), e006548.
37. Good Judgment, "Post-Mortem: Lessons learned in superforecasting: The

Russian invasion of Ukraine," https://goodjudgment.com/wp-content/uploads/2022/03/1570-Post-Mortem-v2.pdf
38. Marshall, G. (2015). *Don't Even Think About It: Why Our Brains Are Wired to Ignore Climate Change*. Bloomsbury Publishing.
39. Horx. "Mein 'Facebook-failure,'" https://www.horx.com/zukunftsforschung/mein-facebook-failure/; Sorrel, C., "More Ballmer Madness: 'There's no chance that the iPhone is going to get any significant market share,'" Wired, 1 May 2007, https://www.wired.com/2007/05/more-ballmer-ma/
40. Wright, R. (2004). *A Short History of Progress*. House of Anansi Press.
41. Torres, P., "How religious and non-religious people view the apocalypse," *The Bulletin*, 18 August 2017, https://thebulletin.org/2017/08/how-religious-and-non-religious-people-view-the-apocalypse/
42. Pew Research Center, "Jesus Christ's return to Earth," 14 July 2010, https://www.pewresearch.org/fact-tank/2010/07/14/jesus-christs-return-to-earth/
43. Pauly, L., "Has the pandemic changed views on human extinction?", YouGov, 16 February 2022, https://yougov.co.uk/topics/politics/articles-reports/2022/02/16/has-pandemic-changed-views-human-extinction
44. Alper, B. A., "How religion intersects with Americans' views on the environment," Pew Research Center, 17 November 2022, https://www.pewresearch.org/religion/2022/11/17/how-religion-intersects-with-americans-views-on-the-environment/#h-end-times-beliefs-and-concern-about-climate-change
45. TZ, "Umfrage zum Weltuntergang: Will Kabel Eins uns für dumm verkaufen?", 9 April 2018, https://www.tz.de/tv/kabel-eins-macht-umfrage-zum-weltuntergang-zr-9763576.html
46. Gaub, F. (2021). "How the Islamic State Sees the Future," EU Institute for Security Studies, Brief, https://www.iss.europa.eu/content/how-islamic-state-sees-future
47. Kermode, F. (1966). "The New Apocalyptists." *Partisan Review*, *XXXIII*(3), 339–361.
48. Harrison, J. F. C. (1979). *The Second Coming: Popular Millenarianism 1780–1850*. Routledge.
49. Roberts, A. (2020). *It's the End of the World: But what are we really afraid of?*, 7. Elliot & Thompson.

50. Hegel, G. F. W. (1924). *Vorlesungen über die Geschichte der Philosophie*. Reclam.
51. Marx, K. (1845). *Theses on Feuerbach*.
52. Catanus, A.-M. "Official and Unofficial Futures of the Communism System: Romanian Futures Studies between Control and Dissidence" and Sommer, V. "Forecasting the Post-Socialist Future: Prognostika in Late Socialist Czechoslovakia, 1970–1989." In Andersson, J., & Rindzeviciute, E. (eds) (2015). *The Struggle for the Long Term in Transnational Science and Politics: Forging the Future*. Routledge.
53. Flax, J., "How to see the future (and know it when you see it)," *Wharton Magazine*, Spring 2016, https://magazine.wharton.upenn.edu/issues/spring-2016/how-to-see-the-future-and-know-it-when-you-see-it/
54. Plomin, R. (2018). *Blueprint: How DNA Makes Us Who We Are*, p. 298. Penguin Books.
55. Ministry of Commerce of the People's Republic of China, "Chinese customs, superstitions and traditions," 29 November 2009, http://us.mofcom.gov.cn/article/aboutchina/202011/20201103012645.shtml#:~:text=Other%20customs%20and%20superstitions%20include,and%201pm%20quarrels%20will%20ensue
56. NASA, "Constellations and the Calendar: Did you recently hear that NASA changed the zodiac signs? Nope, we definitely didn't...", 2020, https://nasa.tumblr.com/post/150688852794/zodiac
57. Zarka, P. (2009). "Astronomy and Astrology." *Proceedings of the International Astronomical Union*, 5(S260), 420–425; McGrew, J. H., & McFall, R. M. (1990). "A Scientific Inquiry into the Validity of Astrology." *Journal of Scientific Exploration*, 4(1), 75–83.
58. Gecewicz, C., "'New Age' beliefs common among both religious and nonreligious Americans", Pew Research Center, 1 October 2018, https://www.pewresearch.org/fact-tank/2018/10/01/new-age-beliefs-common-among-both-religious-and-nonreligious-americans/. Statista, "Glauben männer und frauen an astrologie und horoskope?", https://de.statista.com/statistik/daten/studie/668629/umfrage/umfrage-zum-glauben-an-astrologie-und-horoskope-in-deutschland-nach-geschlecht/
59. American Federation of Certified Psychics and Mediums.
60. Carroll, J., "Thirteen percent of Americans bothered to stay on hotels' 13th floor," Gallup, 15 March 2007, https://news.gallup.com/poll/26887/thirteen-percent-americans-bothered-stay-hotels-13th-floor.aspx
61. Pérez, C. & Votka, S., "What do the tarot cards say? In a pandemic, the

answer might be on Zoom," *Vogue*, 1 September 2020, https://www.vogue.com/article/tarot-card-readings-pandemic-growth

62. Vyse, S. A. (2020). *Superstition: A Very Short Introduction*. Oxford University Press.
63. Dickson, D. H., & Kelly, I. W. (1985). "The 'Barnum Effect' in Personality Assessment: A Review of the Literature." *Psychological Reports*, 57(1), 367–382.
64. Clobert, M., et al. (2016) "Good Day for Leos: Horoscope's Influence on Perception, Cognitive Performances, and Creativity." *Personality and Individual Differences*, 101, 348–355.
65. Podmore, F. (1906). *Robert Owen: A Biography Vol. II*, pp. 604–605. Hutchinson & Co. Spence, L. (2003). *Encyclopedia of Occultism and Parapsychology,* 679. Kessinger Publishing Company.
66. Pronin, E., et al. (2006). "Everyday Magical Powers: The Role of Apparent Mental Causation in the Overestimation of Personal Influence." *Journal of Personality and Social Psychology, 91*, 218–231.
67. Kaku, K. (1975). "Increased Induced Abortion Rate in 1966, an Aspect of a Japanese Folk Superstition", *Annals of Human Biology, 2*(2), 111–115. Kim, Y. S. "Fertility of the Korean Population in Japan Influenced by a Folk Superstition in 1966." *Journal of Biosocial Science, 11*(4), 457–464.
68. Helgert, J. (2020). "The Validity of Astrological Predictions on Marriage and Divorce: A Longitudinal Analysis of Swedish Register Data." *Genus*, 76(34).
69. Rashid, T., "Financial astrologers gaze at stock markets in the stars", *Financial Times*, 17 October 2007, https://www.ft.com/content/98b10826-367b-11e3-aaf1-00144feab7de
70. Andersson, I., et al. (2022). "Even the Stars Think that I Am Superior: Personality, Intelligence and Belief in Astrology." *Personality and Individual Differences*, 187(0), 111389.

5. TROUBLESHOOTING

1. Watkins Jr., J. E., "What might happen in the next hundred years," *Ladies Home Journal*, https://www.personal.psu.edu/staff/t/w/twa101/whatmayhappen.pdf
2. Abohela, I., & Lavin, N. M. (2020). "The Height of Future Architecture: Significance of High versus Low Rise Architecture in Science Fiction Films." *Applied Science University Journal*, 4(2), 57–66.

3. Sheehy, G. (1976). *Passages: Predictable Crises of Adult Life*. Bantam Books.
4. Ware, B. (2012). *The Top Five Regrets of the Dying: A Life Transformed by the Dearly Departing*. Hay House.
5. "Statistics on Mental Trauma", https://fherehab.com/trauma/statistics
6. Duggan, C., et al. (2016). "Resilience and Happiness After Spinal Cord Injury: A Qualitative Study." *Topics in Spinal Cord Injury Rehabilitation*, 22(2), 99–110.
7. Beck, A. T., et al. (1979). *Cognitive Therapy of Depression*. Guilford Press. Abramson, L. Y., et al. (1989). "Hopelessness Depression: A Theory-Based Subtype of Depression." *Psychological Review*, 96(2), 358–372. MacLeod, A. K., et al. (1993). "Components of Hopelessness about the Future in Parasuicide." *Cognitive Therapy and Research*, 17(5), 441–455. Sarkohi, A. (2011). "Future Thinking and Depression." *Linköping studies in Behavioural Science, 160*, https://www.diva-portal.org/smash/get/diva2:458333/FULLTEXT01.pdf. Bjärehed, J., et al. (2010). "Less Positive or More Negative? Future-Directed Thinking in Mild to Moderate Depression." *Cognitive Behaviour Therapy*, 39(1), 37–45. MacLeod, A. K., & Conway, C. (2007). "Well-Being and Positive Future Thinking for the Self Versus Others." *Cognition and Emotion*, 21(5), 1114–1124. Melges, F. T. (1972). "Future Oriented Psychotherapy." *American Journal of Psychotherapy*, 26(1), 22–33.
8. National Institute of Mental Health, "Major Depression," https://www.nimh.nih.gov/health/statistics/major-depression
9. Luppa, M., et al. (2012). "Age- and Gender-Specific Prevalence of Depression in Latest-Life—Systematic Review and Meta-Analysis." *Journal of Affective Disorders, 136*(3), 212–221. https://doi.org/10.1016/j.jad.2010.11.033. Kruijshaar, M. E., et al. (2005). "Lifetime Prevalence Estimates of Major Depression: An Indirect Estimation Method and a Quantification of Recall Bias." *European Journal of Epidemiology, 20*(1), 103–111, https://doi.org/10.1007/s10654-004-1009-0. Novick, D., et al. (2017). "Recovery in Patients with Major Depressive Disorder (MDD): Results of a 6-Month, Multinational, Observational Study." *Patient Preference and Adherence, 31*(11), 1859–1868. Anne, M., & Janssen, S. M. J. (2020). "Relations Between Cultural Life Scripts, Individual Life Stories, and Psychological Distress." *Psychological Reports*, 124(2).
10. World Health Organisation. "Depression," https://www.who.int/news-room/fact-sheets/detail/depression
11. World Health Organisation, "COVID-19 pandemic triggers 25% increase

in prevalence of anxiety and depression worldwide," March 2022, https://www.who.int/news/item/02-03-2022-covid-19-pande mic-triggers-25-increase-in-prevalence-of-anxiety-and-depression-worldwide
12. Ohlis, A., et al. (2022). "Långtidsuppföljning av barn med uppgivenhetssyndrom [Long-Term Outcome of Children Diagnosed with Resignation Syndrome in the Stockholm Region 2005–2012]." *Lakartidningen, 119*, 21171.
13. US Department of Justice, Office of Justice Programmes, "Bureau of Justice statistics: Mental health problems of prison and jail inmates", September 2006, NCJ 213600, https://bjs.ojp.gov/content/pub/pdf/mhppji.pdf
14. Council of Europe, "Prisons and probation: A Council of Europe White Paper on the management of offenders with mental health disabilities and disorders," 9 November 2021, https://rm.coe.int/pc-cp-2021-8-e-rev-2-prisons-and-probation-a-council-of-europe-white-p/1680a47eff
15. Toch, H., et al. (eds). (2018). *Living on Death Row: The Psychology of Waiting to Die*. American Psychological Association. Bradford, C. D. (2011). "Waiting to Die, Dying to Live: An Account of the Death Row Phenomenon from a Legal Viewpoint." *IDJHRL, 5*, 85–92.
16. Hidaka, B. H. (2012). "Depression as a Disease of Modernity: Explanations for Increasing Prevalence." *Journal for Affective Disorders, 140*(3), 205–214. Murphy, J. M., et al. (2000). "A 40-Year Perspective on the Prevalence of Depression: The Stirling County Study." *Archives of General Psychiatry, 57*(3), 209–215. World Health Organization, "Depression and Other Common Mental Disorders: Global Health Estimates", January 2017, https://www.who.int/publications/i/item/depression-global-health-estimates
17. Yokoya, S., et al. (2018). "A Brief Survey of Public Knowledge and Stigma Towards Depression." *Journal of Clinical Medicine Research, 10*(3), 202–209.
18. Herrman, H., et al., "Time for united action on depression: a Lancet–World Psychiatric Association Commission", *The Lancet*, February 2022, https://www.thelancet.com/journals/lancet/article/PIIS0140-6736(21)02141-3/fulltext
19. Wilson, C., "Fresh ideas about the causes of depression are bringing new treatments", *New Scientist*, 18 January 2023, https://www.newscientist.com/article/mg25734220-100-fresh-ideas-about-the-causes-of-depression-are-bringing-new-treatments/
20. Furchtlehner, L. M., et al. (2020). "A Comparative Study of the Efficacy of

Group Positive Psychotherapy and Group Cognitive Behavioral Therapy in the Treatment of Depressive Disorders: A Randomized Controlled Trial." *The Journal of Positive Psychology*, 15(6), 832–845. Asgharipoor, N., et al. (2012). "A Comparative Study on the Effectiveness of Positive Psychotherapy and Group Cognitive-Behavioral Therapy for the Patients Suffering from Major Depressive Disorder." *Iranian Journal of Psychiatry and Behavioral Sciences,* 6(2), 33–41. Lesse, S. (1971). "Future Oriented Psychotherapy—A Prophylactic Technique." *The American Journal of Psychotherapy*, 25(2), 180–193.
21. Vilhauer, J. (2014). *Think Forward to Thrive: How to Use the Mind's Power of Anticipation to Transcend Your Past and Transform Your Life.* New World Library. Melges, F. T. (1982). *Time and the Inner Future: Temporal Approach to Psychiatric Disorders.* Wiley.
22. Furr, N. (2022). *The Upside of Uncertainty: A Guide to Finding Possibility in the Unknown.* Harvard Business Review Press.
23. OECD, "Foresight and anticipatory governance in practice: Lessons in effective foresight institutionalisation", 2021, https://www.oecd.org/strategic-foresight/ourwork/Foresight_and_Anticipatory_Governance.pdf
24. Merton, R. K. (1948). "The Self-Fulfilling Prophecy." *The Antioch Review,* 8(2), 193–210.
25. Aerzteblatt, "Nocebo phenomena in medicine: Their relevance in everyday clinical practice," 2012, https://www.aerzteblatt.de/int/archive/article/127210
26. Van Tongeren, D. R., et al. (2018), "Heroic Helping: The Effects of Priming Superhero Images on Prosociality." *Frontiers in Psychology*, 9, Article 2243.
27. YouGov, "International poll: most expect to feel impact of climate change, many think it will make us extinct," 15 September 2019, https://yougov.co.uk/topics/politics/articles-reports/2019/09/15/international-poll-most-expect-feel-impact-climate
28. Hickman, C., "Climate anxiety in children and young people and their beliefs about government responses to climate change: a global survey," *The Lancet*, December 2021, https://www.thelancet.com/journals/lanplh/article/PIIS2542-5196(21)00278-3/fulltext
29. Live Science, "Could climate change make humans go extinct?", 30 August 2021, https://www.livescience.com/climate-change-humans-extinct.html
30. *Forbes*, "53% Of U.S. adults don't fear growing old—Study finds people

actually fear less as they age," 19 October 2022, https://www.forbes.com/health/medicare/fear-of-aging-survey/#:~:text=Fewer%20Than%20Half%20of%20U.S.,each%20year%20they%20grow%20older

31. Martin, B. (1982). "The Global Health Effects of Nuclear War." *Current Affairs Bulletin*, *59*(7), 14–26. National Research Council (U.S.), "Long-term worldwide effects of multiple nuclear-weapons detonations," Washington, DC, 1975; Martin, B. (1982). "Critique of Nuclear Extinction." *Journal of Peace Research*, *19*(4), 287–300.

32. Rubin, D., et al. (2009). "The Normative and the Personal Life: Individual Differences in Life Scripts and Life Story Events among USA and Danish Undergraduates." *Memory*, *17*(1), 54–68.

33. Bowerman, M. "These Are the Top 10 Bucket List Items on Singles' Lists," *USA Today*, 18 May, 2017, https://www.usatoday.com/story/life/nation-now/2017/05/15/these-top-10-bucket-list-items-singles-lists/319931001

34. Haque, S., & Haskin, P. (2010). "Life Scripts for Emotionally Charged Autobiographical Memories: A Cultural Explanation of the Reminiscence Bump." *Memory*, *18*(7), 712–729. Erdoğan, A., et al. (2008). "On the Persistence of Positive Events in Life Scripts." *Applied Cognitive Psychology*, *22*(1), 95–111.

35. Hatiboğlu, N., & Habermas, T. (2016). "The Normativity of Life Scripts and Its Relation with Life Story Events Across Cultures and Sub-Cultures." *Memory*, *24*, 1369–1381.

36. Coleman, J. T. (2014). "Examining the Life Script of African-Americans: A Test of the Cultural Life Script." *Applied Cognitive Psychology, 28*, 419–426.

37. Keuleers, E., et al. (2015). "Word Knowledge in the Crowd: Measuring Vocabulary Size and Word Prevalence in a Massive Online Experiment." *Quarterly Journal of Experimental Psychology, 68*(8), 1665–1692.

38. Cattell, R. (1971). *Abilities: Their Structure, Growth, and Action*. Houghton Mifflin.

39. Hartshorne, J. K., & Germine, L. T. (2015). "When Does Cognitive Functioning Peak? The Asynchronous Rise and Fall of Different Cognitive Abilities Across the Life Span." *Psychological Science, 26*(4), 433–443; Vaci, N., et al. (2019). "Large Data and Bayesian Modeling-Aging Curves of NBA Players." *Behavior Research Methods, 51*(4), 1544–1564.

40. Waldinger, R. (2023). *The Good Life: Lessons from the World's Longest Study on Happiness*. Rider.

41. Kahneman, D., et al. (1991). "Anomalies: The Endowment Effect, Loss Aversion, and Status Quo Bias." *Journal of Economic Perspectives, 5*(1), 193–206. Eidelman, S., & Crandall, C. S. (2012). "Bias in Favor of the Status Quo." *Social and Personality Psychology Compass, 6*(3). Samuelson, W., & Zeckhauser, R. (1988). "Status quo bias in decision making." *Journal of Risk and Uncertainty, 1*, 7–59.
42. Niemiec, C., et al. (2009). "The Path Taken: Consequences of Attaining Intrinsic and Extrinsic Aspirations in Post-College Life." *Journal of Research in Personality, 43*(3), 291–306.
43. Waldinger, R. (2023). *The Good Life: Lessons from the World's Longest Study on Happiness*. Rider.
44. Niemiec, C., et al. (2009). "The Path Taken: Consequences of Attaining Intrinsic and Extrinsic Aspirations in Post-College Life." *Journal of Research in Personality, 43*(3), 291–306.

6. YOUR FUTURE WARRANTY

1. Library of Congress Legislative Reference Service, "Erroneous predictions and negative comments concerning exploration, territorial expansion, scientific and technological development", May 1969.
2. Jacobsen, M. H., & Tester. K. (eds) (2012). *Utopia: Social Theory and the Future*. Ashgate Publishing.
3. Niemiec, C. (2009). "The Path Taken: Consequences of Attaining Intrinsic and Extrinsic Aspirations in Post-College Life." *Journal of Research in Personality, 43*(3), 291–306.
4. MacAskill, W. (2022). *What We Owe the Future*. Oxford University Press.
5. Rosnick, D. (2013). "Reduced work hours as a means of slowing climate change," Center for Economic and Policy Research, http://www.cepr.net/documents/publications/climate-change-workshare-2013-02.pdf. La Libre, "Inondations: 590 millions d'euros pris en charge par les assurances," August 2021, https://www.lalibre.be/economie/conjoncture/2021/08/12/inondations-590-millions-deuros-pris-en-charge-par-les-assurances-ULWSHH3TYJGA3OIW2JVFHGSIP4/
6. Vaughan, A., "Net-zero living: How your day will look in a carbon-neutral world", *New Scientist*, 1 September 2021, https://www.newscientist.com/article/mg25133504-300-net-zero-living-how-your-day-will-look-in-a-carbon-neutral-world/. Li, G., "Futuristic farm may use 250 times less water than normal", *New Scientist*, 29 September 2021, https://www.

newscientist.com/article/mg25133540-200-futuristic-farm-may-use-250-times-less-water-than-normal/. Klein, A., "New plastic made from DNA is biodegradable and easy to recycle," *New Scientist*, 20 November 2021, https://www.newscientist.com/article/2298314-new-plastic-made-from-dna-is-biodegradable-and-easy-to-recycle/. Howgego, J., "The end of waste: The grand plan to build a truly circular economy", *New Scientist*, 9 February 2022, https://www.newscientist.com/article/mg25333730-800-the-end-of-waste-the-grand-plan-to-build-a-truly-circular-economy/
7. Milkman, K. (2021). *How to Change: The Science of Getting from Where You Are to Where You Want to Be*. Penguin.
8. Torrance, E. P. (1993). "The Beyonders in a Thirty-Year Longitudinal Study of Creative Achievement." *Roeper Review*, *15*(3), 131–135.